UNEX

C000076298

MY!

<u>2 Books In 1</u>

Unexplained Mysteries Of The World,
Bigfoot & The Other Ones

By Brian Kingsley

Main Table of Contents

UNEXPLAINED MYSTERIES OF THE WORLD

A Non-Fiction Collection About
True Hauntings, Lost Civilizations,
Alien Contact & Other Paranormal Enigmas

By Brian Kingsley

Table of Contents

Introduction

Humanity has come so far and explored so much. As a species, we have more or less conquered the entire Earth and all of its resources. We have built towering structures, intricate systems and settled everywhere — from the tallest peaks to the deepest valleys.

We have now entered what many like to think of as the enlightened, scientific era — where old superstitions and fears have been abolished, and the mysteries of the past have been solved. Basically, many of us like to think we have figured it all out.

However, whether we want to admit it or not, we are still surrounded by plenty of enigmas. Unexplained phenomena, such as confirmed instances of remote viewing or sightings of strange beings like Bigfoot, may sow a seed of doubt in even the surest of individuals.

While some sneer at, or shy away from, the thought of investigating the mysterious, there are also those who feel curious, maybe even energized, at the thought of exploring something completely new.

As Neil Armstrong once said:

"Mystery creates wonder, and wonder is the basis for man's desire to understand".

If you are one of those who seek to feel wonder, this book is for you. Herein you will find a varied collection of some of the most intriguing unexplained mysteries of our time.

From the puzzling artifacts of a lost civilization, to psychic visions and shocking UFO landings — by the end of this book, you will have plenty of captivating questions to ponder and investigate further.

Chapter 1

The Riddle of the Sphinx

"What goes on four legs in the morning, two legs at midday, and three legs in the evening?"

This was the question asked by the Sphinx as she prowled the outskirts of the Grecian city of Thebes, according to the ancient playwright Sophocles in his famous tragedy *Oedipus the King*. If the question was answered wrongly – death.

Thankfully for Thebes, the hero of the play answers correctly: "Man," who crawls in infancy, walks upright in maturity, and carries a cane in old age. The Sphinx then hurls herself into the sea and Thebes rejoices.

Although the word 'sphinx' itself very likely derives from the Greek *sphíngō* — meaning 'strangler' or 'to tighten', it was through sea-trade with the Egyptians that the mythical creature found its way to the Hellenic world — gaining a pair of wings and a lousy disposition as it went.

And it is the famous Egyptian rendition that we think of today: The Great Sphinx of Giza. It is silent, staring across time and space. What can we learn of its mysteries?

Ironically enough, when Grecian occupation of Egypt was at its height (during the Ptolemaic dynasties) the Sphinx of Giza was probably buried at least up to its neck in sand.

Although the ancient writer Herodotus considered the Great Pyramid at Giza to be a 'wonder of the world', he made no mention of the Sphinx at all.

In fact, for the majority of its history it has been obscured by sands, only to be uncovered again in 1905. It then captured the imagination of the world, and a debate began which rages to this day: how old is the Sphinx, really?

The established view contends that the Great Sphinx was built during the Fourth Dynasty (around 2613 – 2494 BCE) for either pharaoh Khufu, Djedefra, or Khafre.

This timeframe is again narrowed down by Egyptologists Zahi Hawass and Mark Lehner, who single out Khafre (owner of the nearby second-tallest pyramid at Giza) as both client and model for the statue's face. But does this actually hold up to scrutiny?

It's worth noting there are no inscriptions from the time linking Khafre with the Sphinx – this attribution derives largely from the positioning of the Sphinx (in front of the 'pyramid of Khafre'), a statue of Khafre found buried upside-down in the nearby Valley Temple, and the 'Dream Stele'.

This rather circumstantial proof has led to an ongoing debate over the Sphinx's age, with Khafre-critics offering alternative views that range from the reasonable to the downright ludicrous. While none are wholly convincing in and of themselves, there are several holes in the 'official' story.

The aforementioned 'Dream Stele' – a large stone tablet placed between the paws of the Sphinx – includes only *part* of Khafre's name (Khaf), and even this syllable had flaked off by 1925 when the Stele was again excavated.

There were Egyptologists at the time who interpreted the Stele as referring to Khafre's *excavation* of the Sphinx, rather than his association with building it.

On the other hand, the 'Inventory Stele' (another ancient stone tablet discovered in Egypt) states that Khufu (Khafre's father) made restorations to the head of the Sphinx — implying that it had been there long before. Conservative Egyptologists point out that the 'Inventory Stele' was inscribed over a thousand years after the reigns of both Khufu and Khafre... but so too was the 'Dream Stele'.

The head of the Sphinx is not only a little out of proportion – it's a *lot* out of proportion. But the ancient Egyptians were renowned stonemasons and artisans, so why should this be the case? Has it been re-carved?

Similarly, large-scale propaganda projects would be undertaken by later Dynasties: Queen Hatshepsut almost never made it to the history books, after nearly all mention of her name was destroyed by succeeding rulers Thutmose III and Amenhotep II.

Also (although in this case while trying to institute monotheism) Akhenaten ordered all mentions of the rival god Amon wiped out. Could Khafre merely have laid claim to the Sphinx, not actually overseen the building of it?

The idea that water erosion was a significant factor in determining the Sphinx's age entered the public domain via *The Mystery of the Sphinx* — a documentary which showcased the work of John Anthony West and geologist Robert Schoch.

Despite receiving a lot of criticism from establishment figures, West and Schoch's work received independent verification from English geologist Colin Reader.

Although arriving at significantly later dates than Schoch (who had proposed a 5000 – 10,000 BCE date for construction), Reader still concluded that the Sphinx predated both Khufu's and Khafre's constructions by several hundred years, placing it in the Early Dynastic Period.

Yet another independent study (performed by geologist David Coxhill) suggested a pre-Dynastic construction date. Could the Sphinx actually pre-date the pyramids?

All three studies also concluded it was built at the same time as the nearby Valley and Sphinx Temples, which were later expanded upon by the redevelopment efforts of Khufu, Khafre & co.

Interestingly, these temples (Valley and Sphinx) feature a style of masonry that differs from the surrounding Giza plateau, typified by particularly large, undressed limestone megaliths, some weighing over 200 tons – significantly larger than those used in regular temple construction.

This specific style of masonry is also shared by the Osireion — an enigmatic chapel connected to the temple of Seti I at Abydos. Were all three built around the same time as the Sphinx?

Here's where things get even murkier. Remember the 'establishment' figure, Zahi Hawass? As admirable as his efforts may be on one level, he also has a somewhat checkered past. Hawass, Chief Inspector of the Giza Pyramid Plateau, resigned briefly from his position in 1993 (though there are claims he was fired for a scandal involving a theft from a hidden 'door' in the Great Pyramid).

Either way, he was eventually re-instated in '94, promoted to Director of the Giza Plateau in '98, and in 2002 became the Secretary General of the Egyptian Supreme Council of Antiquities. He has been accused of blocking archaeological digs and stopping progress in general on any projects but his own, all the while being a reality TV star (on his own show: *Chasing Mummies*) and pocketing $200,000 a year for being National Geographic's 'explorer-in-residence'.

In 2011, amidst a debacle involving contracts, the Egyptian Museum gift shop, and a company he had holdings in, Zahi Hawass was sentenced to a year in prison. However, the jail sentence would be lifted the very next day.

Meanwhile, during that same month in London, Hawass' line of "khakis, denim shirts and carefully worn leather jackets" went on sale at the Harrod's department store.

By July, the Egyptian government had been turned over, and Hawass 'resigned' from his position – although there are numerous accounts (one filmed) from co-workers that stated he was sacked amid a torrent of abuse. Apparently, some people had wanted him gone for a while.

Somewhere among this drama, there were consistent rumors of underground digs being carried out, at night, beneath the Giza plateau. There was also a video uploaded to Youtube, which was taken down shortly after, of objects being carted away in the darkness to be taken to a nearby airport.

Then, in 2009, six men died when an illegal tunnel collapsed beneath the Giza plateau, not too far from the Sphinx. Allegations of state funding and

momentous finds were whispered among
independent researchers and archeology enthusiasts.

Conspiracy gibberish? Perhaps. But there does seem
to be something strange going on underneath Giza,
and Hawass hasn't helped clarify matters by making
several contradictory statements to the press and on
his blog about the presence of underground tunnels.

The area has always been known to be riddled with
caves. After all, Giza's ancient name was *Rostau*,
meaning the 'mouth of passages'. But could it lead
beneath the Sphinx? To the Hall of Records?

Famous alleged psychic, Edgar Cayce (known as the
'sleeping prophet'), once predicted that one of the
three Atlantean Halls of Records would be found
beneath the Sphinx (more on that in chapter 9).
Similar Atlantean origins have been claimed of the
statue itself.

Although such an idea is tantalizing, researchers have
not yet managed to amass enough evidence to
support it. But there are indeed several clues to the
Great Riddle, scattered through the pre-history which
we are still uncovering:

1. Aker, an ancient Egyptian deity known from at least the First Dynasty, represented the horizon. He was depicted as a lion, and protected the sun god when he first entered the netherworld.

   Was the early Giza site the home of a solar lion cult, like Colin Reader believes? Did the original Sphinx have the head of a lion? And was the cult located underneath Giza?

2. *Nabta Playa* was an important ceremonial center in southern Egypt for Saharan nomadic peoples from at least 12,000 years ago. Evidence of cult worship begins to emerge around the 6th millennium BCE. Stone calendar circles which echo Stonehenge, but predate it by 2000 years, show that the people there closely observed the stars.

3. The *Löwenmensch* figurine is a prehistoric sculpture found in Germany. It has a humanoid shape, but a lion's head. It has been dated as far back as circa 40,000 BCE.

4. When the 11,000-year-old site at Gobekli Tepe in Turkey was discovered, the British newspaper The Guardian finished their coverage of the find with a quote from Vecihi

Ozkaya, the director of a nearby dig at Kortiktepe:

(While pointing to a photo of a half-human, half-lion statuette)

"Look at this... It's a sphinx, thousands of years before Egypt. South-eastern Turkey, northern Syria — this region saw the wedding night of our civilization."

Despite message boards buzzing (and the passage of almost a decade) no one seems to be able to find a picture, or indeed any further reference to this mysterious proto-sphinx. Was it an archaeologist exaggerating? Or was it perhaps something we're not supposed to see?...

Either way, the Riddle of the Sphinx continues to baffle both academics and independent researchers alike. As new clues are being uncovered year by year, piece by piece, we can only wonder what the future will reveal about the lion-bodied enigma of the ancient desert.

Chapter 2

The Mothman Cometh

On January 17, 1909, an unidentified winged creature was reported throughout the American state of New Jersey. Over the next five days, hundreds of sightings, across more than thirty towns, were published in newspapers.

This prompted the closure of several schools in the Delaware valley. Farmers set steel traps in the fields while hunters attempted to track the beast. "The Jersey Devil" was on the loose, it was said.

Police officer James Sackville, one of the first recorded witnesses, claimed to have seen the creature during a routine patrol in Bristol, Pennsylvania on the 17th. He heard dogs barking around 2AM and went to investigate, only to find himself confronted by a large, winged entity with strange features.

It reportedly emitted a terrible scream right before Sackville ran towards it while firing his weapon. Strangely enough, the creature looked to be unmoved by the hail of bullets. After a moment of silence, it flew off, without a single visible gun wound.

Despite the weirdness of his story, most locals saw James Sackville as an honorable man who they could trust. This was demonstrated by the fact that he later became Bristol's chief of police. Sackville insisted that his encounter with the so-called Jersey Devil was real, and stood by the story until his last days.

In the hundred years since the rash of Jersey Devil sightings, various theories have been put forward as explanation: mass hysteria, an unknown species of animal, a humungous sandhill crane, an extraterrestrial, a pterosaur, or even the demonic 13th child of one 'Mother Leeds'.

The 'Devil' continues to be seen up to the present day in and around the state of New Jersey, but creatures of its kind have also been reported across the globe. Over 50 years after the infamous 1909 sightings, another wave of winged monster reports would sweep the nearby state of West Virginia — the "Mothman" had left his mark.

The local newspaper, *Point Pleasant Register,* carried an unusual article on November 16, 1966 titled: "Couples See Man-Sized Bird... Creature... Something".

Although it was somewhat light on details, it was the first published report of what would soon be known as 'Mothman', and would find fuller account in John Keel's popular book on the subject, *The Mothman Prophecies.*

On the night before the historic article was published, between 11:30PM and midnight, Roger and Linda Scarberry were driving through a region known to locals as the 'TNT Area' together with another couple they knew. 6 miles north of Point Pleasant, and situated within the McClintic Wildlife Management Area, the TNT area used to be the site of ordinance and explosive manufacture during World War II.

Now, it was a teenage hangout — a venue known for dirt-road drag races, lovers' lanes, and the occasional police patrol. That night, however, the two couples, cruising in the Scarberry's '57 Chevrolet, saw no one else on the lonely back roads.

Linda was the first to notice something as they slowed down near an old power plant: two bright-red circles "about two inches in diameter and six inches apart". Roger stopped the car, and all four soon understood that the circles were attached to a larger figure, perhaps an animal of some sort.

Roger recalled:

"It was shaped like a man, but bigger... Maybe six and a half or even seven feet tall. And it had big wings folded against its back."

The couples stared transfixed at the creature's eyes

before it turned slowly away from them and shuffled towards the power plant. Steve Mallette yelled from the back seat and Roger stepped hard on the accelerator, heading for the nearby Route 62.

They passed a hill by the side of the road and saw the thing again (or another one like it) spread its wings and rise straight up in the air "like a helicopter". Roger pulled onto Route 62 in an effort to outrun it.

He later stated:

"We were doing one hundred miles an hour and that bird kept right up with us. It wasn't even flapping its wings."

Mary Mallette heard it making a squeaking sound "like a big mouse". It finally stopped following them as they neared the city limits. Heading straight to Mason County courthouse, they poured into the sheriff's station in the early hours of the morning, relaying their story to Deputy Millard Halstead.

The visibly-shaken couples went back to where they saw the creature along with the deputy and city police, but could find no apparent evidence. Dozens of locals drove out to the TNT area the next day, armed with guns and eager to catch or kill whatever monstrosity had been seen the night before.

However, no Mothman could be found.

A woman named Marcella Bennett also witnessed the terrifying winged being. She was only about half a mile away from the aspiring monster hunters when it took place, but her story would not be published until the next day. Sitting in her parked car, she noticed a figure several feet behind her in the darkness.

"It seemed as if it had been lying down... It rose up slowly from the ground. A big gray thing. Bigger than a man, with terrible glowing red eyes," she said.

Mrs. Bennett's friend grabbed her, and they ran inside, locking the door behind them, thinking they were in the clear. After hearing a sound on the porch, however, they became horrified to find that the red eyes were peering at them through the window. The police were immediately called, but the creature had vanished by the time they reached the house.

A wave of Mothman sightings followed after these initial reports, concentrated over the November-December period of 1966, but lasting up until the tragic collapse of the Silver Bridge on December 15th of 1967.

Many of these are catalogued by the writer Gray Barker and, most famously, the previously-mentioned author of *The Mothman Prophecies*, John Keel, who believed that the Mothman functioned as a sort of interdimensional herald of doom.

At the other end of the spectrum, skeptics are quick to point out that the Mothman was little more than a misidentified barn owl or sandhill crane (the latter an explanation also given to the Jersey Devil). However, the huge size difference between these animals and the reported creature casts doubt on these theories.

Ultimately, without physical evidence, we are left

with only eyewitness testimonies, albeit a good number of them. Some of the accounts are admittedly very hard to believe for the average person, but should that really be the test of truth? Should we assume that if someone sees something extraordinary, they have simply misidentified the ordinary?

When the Silver Bridge collapsed and caused the death of 46 people, the Mothman stopped being seen in Point Pleasant. Nevertheless, its close cousins continued to appear the world over. 10 years after the collapse, along the Mexican-American border in Texas, a large, red-eyed, flying entity reportedly wreaked havoc on the local populace for several months.

Besides the mauling of local livestock, the creature allegedly attacked a man named Armando Grimaldo while he was in his mother-in-law's backyard at night. After hearing "a funny kind of whistling" and the flap of wings, Grimaldo was grabbed from above by what he described as "something with big claws."

As he ran for his life, he quickly looked back to see a bird-like being as big as a man, with leathery skin, a strange, bat-like face, and glowing red eyes. It terrorized him, following him around the backyard and shredding some of his clothing.

Finally, he managed to run inside the house where he collapsed exhausted on the floor. He was later taken to the hospital and treated for shock and minor wounds before being released.

More recently, a winged humanoid was reportedly seen in Singapore on three separate occasions in the first week of September, 2015; less than a year before that, the small Argentinian town of Quilino was host to its own flying creature, both being identified as 'Mothman'. What are we to make of these sightings?

John Keel originally subscribed to an extraterrestrial explanation involving UFOs, gradually opening up to a more holistic view of the paranormal. Indeed, Keel linked the Mothman visitations to UFO sightings, men in black encounters, psychic phenomena, and the collapse of the Silver Bridge.

Point Pleasant was an example of what he called a 'window' or 'window area' (Keel was proficient at coining ufological phrases: we also have him to thank for 'waves', 'ultraterrestrials', and even 'men in black').

Cornwall, England was another such 'window' in 1976, bristling with reports of UFOs, a sea creature (called the 'Morgawr Monster') and an 'Owlman' – a large winged hominid with red glowing eyes. Mothman, The Jersey Devil, Owlman... Are they all the same entity?

Noted psychologist Carl Jung might say they were reflections of a basic human archetype. A dark, anthropomorphic figure with red eyes could be interpreted as an encounter with the Shadow archetype, with things we repress.

If we saw a medieval bible with an illustration of such, we'd very likely interpret it as a demon or devil. Is that what Mothman is, then — a modern-day Satan of suburbia? The projected shadow-self of our collective unconscious?

On the other hand, several of the Mothman encounters suggest a definite, physical presence. As we attempt to understand quantum law and the nature of the 'observer effect', the line between objectivity and subjectivity becomes increasingly blurred. On which side the Mothman sits, we may never know for sure. The answer may even be "both".

Chapter 3

The Great Mass Sighting Of Zimbabwe

On the 16th of September, 1994, a spectacular event took place in Ruwa, Zimbabwe, near the Ariel Elementary School. While most of the faculty were at a meeting, the children were playing outside with only a few adults overseeing them. Suddenly, out of nowhere, the kids started seeing strange things in the sky.

5 large, unidentified flying objects appeared, disappeared and then reappeared above them — as if they shifted in and out of existence. This extraordinary display went on for quite some time, before one of them separated from the rest and landed on a hill, right outside the schoolyard.

In contrast to most UFO sightings, which usually involve only a few people, as many as 62 students from ages 5 to 12 witnessed this astonishing event.

Some of the kids ran to the border fence of the school and observed two dark, humanoid creatures exiting the mysterious craft. According to the children, they were only around 3 feet tall, with thin bodies, what looked to be long, black hair, as well as enormous, almond-shaped, upturned eyes — similar to those of the classical "grey" alien often described in ET encounters and abduction stories.

According to those who were closest to the scene, one of the beings appeared to be moving around the hill as if it was searching for something, while the other one stayed near the UFO. Shortly after, the surveying entity looked towards the school and apparently noticed the children who were staring at it from the other side of the border fence.

As if someone instantly rewound a movie scene, the wandering being then vanished and reappeared near its craft in the blink of an eye. A few seconds later, both of the creatures disappeared, apparently making their way back into their vessel, which then proceeded to hover off the ground before flying away at an incredible speed.

It was later revealed that the creature that was moving about had communicated with the children via telepathy. This took place in the brief moment that they stared at each other.

The message the being relayed made a lasting impact on many of the kids. It reportedly told them that humanity was doing too much damage to the Earth, and that if they did not take proper care of it, the result would be disastrous.

One of the school children remembered one

important detail of this message: that humanity's technological development was too far ahead compared to its spiritual evolution. This was the root of the problem.

After the brief, but intense, experience with the alien beings, some of the children at the Ariel School panicked, and ran towards the faculty crying and shouting for help.

Though the teachers reacted quickly to their distress, they did not buy the fantastical-sounding story, and thought the older kids had played an elaborate prank on the younger ones in order to scare them.

Many of the students were frustrated by their teachers lack of reaction. With the memories fresh in their mind, they rushed straight home after school hours to tell their parents about the incredible event.

A number of the kids were visibly disturbed about what had happened, and would not stop talking about it. Because of this, a group of parents got together and drove to the school in order to clear things up with the faculty.

Rumors of what took place that day quickly spread around the country, and several paranormal researchers took interest in it. Among them was one of Africa's most prominent UFOlogists at the time, Cynthia Hind. She was an experienced field researcher for MUFON (the Mutual UFO Network) — an international organization that specialized in tracking down and documenting potential UFO and ET sightings.

Hind was at the scene of the alleged landing the very next day after it took place, eager to begin her investigation. She was met with a cooperative staff who now realized that something big had indeed happened. Hind asked the headmaster of the Ariel School, Colin Mackie, to isolate the kids and tell them to draw what they had witnessed.

To everyone's amazement, all of the finalized drawings closely resembled each other. Later that day, the UFO researcher interviewed a dozen of the young students one by one. All of their stories seemed to match, with no glaring inconsistencies or contradictions.

While the Ariel School sightings were exceptional in nature, other people had been seeing UFOs in the skies over Zimbabwe two days before the big event. The witnesses, who also included respectable scientists and officials, described what looked like large, metallic discs and breathtaking color displays which could be easily seen in the clear night sky.

Hind wasn't the only notable researcher who investigated the mass sightings in Zimbabwe. Professor of Psychiatry from the Harvard University, and Pulitzer Prize winner, Dr. John Mack, traveled to Africa together with his associate Dominique Callimanopulos in order to search for answers. After arriving at the Ariel School, the two men conducted a series of well-planned interviews with many of the students.

With the help of a South African movie producer named Nicky Carter, they were able to document most of it on videotape. After over a week of careful questioning, the men were able to map out a detailed description of the event, as the common threads between the children's stories became apparent. Mack, Callimanopulos and Carter all came to believe that the kids were telling the truth about what they saw that fateful day.

5 years after conducting his interviews, Dr. John Mack released a book titled *"Passport To The Cosmos: Human Transformation And Alien Encounters"* which included details about the Ariel School event.

Soon after, many of Mack's colleagues started questioning his ability to perform his duties, since he had a strong interest in UFOs and ETs. They managed to convince the heads of Harvard at the time to launch an investigation into his credibility as a professor. More than a year passed before they finally concluded that Mack was sane, and that he would be allowed to continue his work at the university.

Besides writing his own books and articles about the Ariel School incident, John Mack also allowed various films and documentary series to use the footage from his interviews with the children. Among the most prolific of these was the long-running TV show "Unsolved Mysteries".

That would not be the end of it, however, as a filmmaker named Randall Nickerson took interest in the case in the early 2000's. He managed to get a hold of Dominique Callimanopulos, who helped him get permission from Mack to use recordings of his interviews in a documentary. With the most important footage secured, Nickerson traveled to Africa, where he would stay for nine months while working diligently on his film.

While he was there, he managed to locate other witnesses who saw the same kind of UFOs as the kids at the Ariel School. He also did an interview with Tim Leech — a reporter who worked for the BBC and covered the extraordinary event right after it took place.

Finally, Nickerson sought out several of the school children who witnessed the incident first hand in 1994. They were now adults, led busy lives, and most of them had traveled to other parts of the world.

Nonetheless, when interviewed, they all clearly remembered the details of the landing outside their schoolyard. Interestingly, none of their stories had changed, which suggests that something impactful did indeed take place that fateful day.

Chapter 4

The Paranormal Prison

The Eastern State Penitentiary is one of the world's most infamous prisons when it comes to paranormal happenings. It has a dark past, filled with extensive abuse, torture and, some say, even inhuman experiments.

In the old days, the penitentiary was filled with all kinds of criminals. From murderers and rapists to pick-pocketers and shop-lifters, many disheartened souls ended their lives inside the dreaded prison.

When it was first opened in the early 1800's, it was originally intended for rehabilitation purposes instead of the usual, harsh punishment that prisons were known for. This was done by the Christian order known as the Quakers, who wanted to offer the inmates an opportunity to think about their actions and turn towards God for forgiveness.

The religious influence can be seen in the interior of the building, which — with its arched ceilings, large iron gates, and stone walls — clearly took inspiration from medieval churches.

Furthermore, all of the cells initially came with a bible, and the first batch of prisoners found themselves needing to bow whenever entering, due to the low opening of the doors. However, this was later changed to heavier metal doors that were completely covered by wood, in order to drown out the noise from the inmates.

The Eastern State Penitentiary became one of the first prisons in the United States to use solitary confinement. This was largely due to the influence of the aforementioned Quakers, who were convinced of the need for criminals to reflect and repent in solitude.

Because of this, many of those who were imprisoned there spent their whole sentence, sometimes even the remainder of their lives, in more or less complete isolation. Unsurprisingly, this took a heavy toll on many minds.

The penitentiary was constructed to hold around 250 inmates at a time. Due to the initial focus on rehabilitation over punishment, every cell had running water, heat, and its own toilet. According to certain historians, some prisoners were even allowed to play with dogs when they were out in the courtyard.

This somewhat-rosy view of the facility was eventually challenged when the author Charles Dickens went on a visit there during the 1840's. He wrote of horrible living conditions and extremely poor treatment of the inmates.

He described his experience at the Eastern State Penitentiary as follows:

"Looking down these dreary passages, the dull repose and quiet that prevails, is awful. Occasionally, there is a drowsy sound from some lone weaver's shuttle, or shoemaker's last, but it is stifled by the thick walls and heavy dungeon-door, and only serves to make the general stillness more profound.

Over the head and face of every prisoner who comes into this melancholy house, a black hood is drawn; and in this dark shroud, an emblem of the curtain dropped between him and the living world, he is led to the cell from which he never again comes forth, until his whole term of imprisonment has expired. He is a man buried alive — to be dug out in the slow round of years...

...I believe that very few men are capable of estimating the immense amount of torture and agony which this dreadful punishment, prolonged for years, inflicts upon the sufferers".

In early 1913, the penitentiary became too
overcrowded to run efficiently (reportedly housing
around 1700 inmates at the time) and thus it finally
abandoned its solitary confinement program and sent
many people to other prisons. That did not stop the
suffering within the facility, however, as guards and
other officials employed brutal tactics to keep
troublesome inmates in line.

To punish dissenters, they threw freezing water at
them in winter time, frequently starved them,
chained their tongues to their wrists, strapped them
tightly to chairs for days on end, among other things.

As indicated by the half-dug tunnels found underneath the penitentiary, many prisoners desperately tried to find a way out of the torturous existence. However, none of them (including the infamous bank robber William Sutton, who spent 11 years of his life there) managed to fully escape.

Many believe that the penitentiary's brutal procedures caused severe depression and mental illness in most of the inmates that were there for an extended period. Many of them ended up committing suicide, while others carried out beastly murders of their fellow prisoners.

During the 1940's, both the officers and inmates of the facility started reporting feeling a mysterious presence, as well as seeing and hearing ghosts. To most outsiders, however, this was thought of as nothing more than an urban legend.

In 1970, the Eastern State Penitentiary was officially closed down and emptied of its prisoners. It was all but abandoned one year later. Soon after its shutdown, a small forest started growing in the various cell blocks and along the stone walls.

After being cleared of wild growth and stray animals in 1996, it reopened — but this time as a museum available to the general public. To the surprise of employees and visitors alike, it would prove to be anything but an ordinary exhibition.

Shortly after the penitentiary opened its doors to the public, reports of unsettling paranormal activity started coming in. Some told of an ominous, shadowy figure who was frequently spotted in one of the prison's watch towers. Others, of blurry outlines of men that would fade in and out of sight.

Even more terrifying, people heard disembodied voices – blood-curdling screams, loud wailing and desperate calls for help. People have also noticed sounds of footsteps in the empty courtyard, movement in some of the cells, and maniacal laughter in one of the corridors.

Due to its reputation, a good deal of ghost hunters and other paranormal investigators visit the penitentiary every year. Based on the reports that have come in, the cell blocks numbered 4, 6 and 12 seem to have the most paranormal activity — ghostly voices and faces being the most commonly reported phenomena.

Certain researchers have allegedly recorded some of these strange happenings on camera and audio. The most notable example is from the crew of the TV show *Ghosthunters*, who apparently captured footage of a specter moving towards the direction of their camera.

Other paranormal enthusiasts have also recorded supposed EVP's (electronic voice phenomenon) in the building, including unintelligible whispering as well as disembodied voices saying "I'm lonely" and "help me".

Some visitors and employees of the old Philadelphia prison have reportedly had more intimate experiences as well. These include sudden drops in room temperature accompanied with an overwhelming feeling of being watched, invisible hands attempting to push them down stairs, sudden full-body chills, and a head-on encounter with a shadowy figure which then disappeared out of nowhere.

Suffice to say, if there are any places on Earth that are legitimately haunted, the Eastern State Penitentiary certainly seems to fit the bill.

Chapter 5

Göbekli Tepe & Our Veiled Past

A 1963 survey carried out by the universities of Istanbul and Chicago found mysterious archaeological remains atop a plateau in southeast Turkey.

They noted possible Neolithic material, but assumed that the huge limestone slabs in the area were simply Medieval gravestones. 31 years later, an archaeologist named Klaus Schmidt read the '63 survey's brief description of the site and decided to go and have a look for himself.

He arrived at the mound on the plateau where the so-called gravestones were recorded and recognized them for what they potentially were – the tops of megalithic T-shaped pillars, similar to ones unearthed at a dig he'd been working on at nearby Nevalı Çori.

The following year, with the aid of the Turkish Sanhurfa Museum, Schmidt began excavation on the site and found the pillars that he suspected would be there. A new historical wonder had been unearthed – Göbekli Tepe.

Research of the site would come to reveal a number of interesting facts:

1. It is the oldest megalithic structure known so far, dating back 11,000 years. As multiple news websites proclaimed, it is 6,000 years older than the world-famous Stonehenge.

2. The stones from the earliest layer of activity number around 200 and are arranged into circles or 'enclosures'. Two T-shaped pillars stand in the center of each circle – the largest is over 19 feet tall and weighs a whopping 50 tons.

3. It is estimated that only 10% or less of Göbekli Tepe has been excavated so far. It will likely take several decades to uncover all of it.

4. It appears the people who constructed these megaliths hadn't yet undergone the 'Neolithic revolution'. That means they were erected before metal-working, pottery, agriculture, animal domestication, writing, and even the wheel. In other words, as far as current indications go, these people were (or at least, should have been, according to mainstream history) hunter-gatherers.

5. Archaeologists estimate that a group of 500 people would be needed to construct and move just one of the T-shaped pillars. That's a lot of hunter-gatherers to co-ordinate, to put it mildly.

   In terms of societal evolution, humans didn't congregate in such numbers until agriculture forced them to stay put and establish cities. Or at least, that's what we have been told.

6. Enigmatic carvings adorn the stones, some carved in relief with rounded edges. Predominantly, animals are depicted – all are wild, and no pictographic representations of domestication have been found. Portrayal of formidable creatures, such as bears and boars, seems to be favored.

7. The standing stones appear to have been intentionally mass-buried around 8,200 BCE. Nobody knows why.

So, what does Göbekli Tepe show us of the culture who constructed it? As is often the case, there are some conflicting theories. Klaus Schmidt believed (and popular opinion seems to side with him) that it was the world's very first temple.

No evidence of habitation has thus far been found (bear in mind that only around 10% or so has been unearthed), which gives circumstantial evidence to his claim.

In 2015, more weight was lent to this idea by the discovery of a small plaque, measuring 2.3 by 1 inches, showing two distinctive T-shaped pillars flanking a stick figure. Above the figure's head and between the tops of the pillars is a small hole, mirroring the placement of holes found cut in two rectangular blocks inside the enclosures. Taken together, the symbolic layout of both the enclosure at large and the plaque suggests that Schmidt could have been right in his rather bold claim.

However, he also had an even bolder claim: mentioning to a reporter that Göbekli Tepe was in fact a garden in the Eden from the Bible. Not necessarily Eden itself, but in the general vicinity. And it would seem that his idea is not entirely without merit.

According to Schmidt, hunter-gatherer "Göbekli-ans" lived a life of paradise until agriculture and domestication (often referred to as the fruit of knowledge) led to the Fall.

There are also a number of facts that seem to back up this narrative:

1. The advent of human sacrifice is generally associated with cultures that are post-Neolithic revolution (Cayonu, a later agricultural site in the immediate area, contains the earliest evidence of human sacrifice).

2. The bones of Neolithic hunter-gatherer societies have been shown to be much healthier than their immediate agricultural descendants — enjoying longer lives and taller, stronger physiques.

3. The bones also show no difference in health between men and women (which was also soon to change), indicating that societies had no significant gender stratification.

4. The cultivation of wheat very likely began in the area.

5. Though it is now barren, the area was once rich in lush woodlands, rivers, and herds of game before being over-farmed.

On the more mythological front, the evidence is not too shabby, either. For one, the Book of Genesis says Eden was bound by four rivers (two of them being the Tigris and Euphrates) and situated west of Assyria. Göbekli Tepe lies within these very borders.

Furthermore, the word 'Eden' derives from a Sumerian word meaning 'plain' – Göbekli is situated atop a plateau on the Harran Plains. Assyrian texts also mention a kingdom called 'Beth Eden' which was 50 miles away.

Schmidt's general idea of Göbekli Tepe functioning as a temple seems to be gathering strength as more artifacts are unearthed. Still, with so little excavated, it might not pay to get too comfortable with any particular notions... but we can always speculate.

Perhaps one of the most interesting relics unearthed so far is what has been dubbed the 'vulture stone'. Graphically speaking, along with the plaque mentioned earlier, the vulture stone is among the most complex pictograms seen at Göbekli Tepe. It depicts a headless person at the bottom of the stone surrounded by animals (mainly birds). Most prominent are two vultures (one large, one juvenile) and a scorpion.

The biggest vulture, in a stance that suggests anthropomorphism, holds a wing outstretched with a ball (presumably a literal or symbolic representation of the person's missing head) balanced on the wingtip. Although this could be read as either partially or entirely symbolic, there is evidence that perhaps some of the earliest known 'sky burials' were performed in the area.

Sky burial (a funerary practice still around today) involves a human corpse being left atop a mountain or other high place to be eaten by carrion-feeding birds. It may sound rather grim, but the practice underlies Buddhist teachings on impermanence and the sustaining cycle of life/death.

Vultures, specifically, also adorned head-dresses worn by members of female Egyptian royalty, in order to signify their status as divine beings. There is evidence of strange 'bird tombs' in both the Anatolian region of Turkey and the Giza plateau.

Could Göbekli Tepe, then, have been the center for a vulture cult that practiced sky burial? If so, did they also interpret the ritual symbolically? Concrete answers remain elusive.

Göbekli Tepe is situated near the mouth of the Euphrates River and, symbolically enough, further downstream we find Mesopotamia – also known as the 'birthplace of civilization'.

Not that Göbekli Tepe necessarily usurps that title (at least yet) but it *may* provide a window into a proto-culture whose influence not only drifted down to Mesopotamia, Egypt and the Levant, but also further, to the early Indus Valley peoples of the east.

As for sky burials, it is worth noting that dismemberment, ascent and rebirth are all key elements in later Hermetic traditions and Mystery schools, not to mention the role of the Hindu goddess Kali. Was Göbekli Tepe a conduit for the dissemination of these ideas?

As the excavation continues, many are hopeful that we will know the answers to this question, and many more, in the near future.

Chapter 6

The Inexplicable Landing

On the 20th of May, 1967, a man named Stephen Michalak traveled to the Whiteshell Provincial Park — located in the central Canadian province of Manitoba. He was an amateur geologist and passionate outdoorsman, and was quite experienced when it came to prospecting.

Once he reached Whiteshell, he made his way into the wilds to look for potential ores. After trekking for some time, he came upon a promising rocky formation next to the Falcon Lake.

After searching for a while, he finally discovered what looked to be a rich vein of quartz near a small stream. Before he was done checking out the vein, however, he was interrupted by an extraordinary sight — two bright-red lights in the sky which looked to be headed in his direction.

As they came closer, the red lights were shown to be emanating from a couple of big, metallic objects that were shaped much like deep saucers.

The lights started flashing in different colors — from red to orange, orange to grey. Then, one of the UFOs flew down and landed on a large, flat rock, about 150 feet away from the stunned prospector, while the other one stayed hovering silently in the air above.

Michalak estimated that the mysterious craft was around 35 feet across. It looked to be made of extremely polished, high-quality steel, and it had a golden glow to it.

The colored lights continued flashing from the inside of the object — so brightly, in fact, that Michalak's eyes began watering due to the intensity, even though he was wearing a pair of welding glasses. Soon after landing, the craft started giving off a strong, sulfur-like smell.

Then, Michalak heard what he described as a hissing sound, before seeing a small opening appear on the side of the strange vessel. He could hear what sounded like whispers coming from inside of it, which made him suspect that it was some sort of experimental flying machine manned by humans — possibly the Soviets.

Stephen Michalak decided to use his considerable linguistic skills to get a response from the pilots. In Russian, he proceeded to ask the mysterious voices if they spoke the language, but nothing could be heard from within the UFO.

He then asked the same question in Ukrainian, Italian, French, German and English. Still, no answers.

Curious and increasingly impatient, Michalak approached the large object. He peered inside the opening and witnessed what looked like a geometric pattern of bright lights.

They seemed to be flashing in a set sequence above something resembling a control panel. Even though he thought he had heard voices earlier, the craft looked to be without a crew.

Getting closer to the object, Michalak could see that it was not actually made from steel. Instead, it seemed to be made from a glass-like material — the surface was completely smooth and very shiny.

Overcome with curiosity, he finally reached out to touch the craft. To his surprise, the surface was so hot that the fingers of his thick glove immediately started to melt away. Startled, he withdrew his hand. In a matter of seconds, the small opening closed, and the UFO flew straight up into the air at breakneck speed.

At the same time, another small opening appeared (which Michalak perceived to be an exhaust port) and gave off a small, but intense burst of extremely hot air which instantly set his clothing on fire.

Panicked, he trashed around on the ground, ripping off his jacket and shirt before finally stamping out the flames.

Within minutes after doing so, Michalak started feeling severely sick. He marked the place of the UFO landing with some pinecones and branches and began heading back to where he had parked earlier.

As he scrambled through the wilderness, his sickness got worse and worse. When he finally made it to his car, he immediately started driving towards his hotel. The ride would take longer than anticipated, however, as he had to pull over several times to puke.

Worried about his declining health, Michalak weighed his options. He knew that the nearest hospital of Misericordia was over 4 hours from his location. He decided to call his wife and son, and asked them to meet him at a bus station in Winnipeg. After he finally met up with them, they all traveled to the emergency room together.

After the doctors had analyzed him, Michalak was admitted for a huge list of health issues which included diarrhea, fatigue, headaches, dizziness, numbness, swollen joints, burns, skin patches and eye irritation.

Furthermore, Michalak's blood tests showed that his lymphocytes (white blood cells that fight infections) had somehow been lowered to 16%, down from the normal levels of 25% — though they gradually stabilized again during his stay at the hospital. His appetite was also heavily diminished during his recovery period, which made him lose a whole 22 pounds of bodyweight.

The burns on Michalak's chest were closely examined by medical staff, who reported several oddities. For one, they had a geometrical pattern to them, much like a chess board — as if he had fallen onto a searing-hot grill. The marks eventually faded, but then, weirdly enough, they reappeared even more pronounced a day later.

After several doctors had inspected Michalak and his physical readings, they concluded that exposure to high levels of radiation seemed to be the cause of his symptoms. When they tested him, however, the results came back negative — there were no traces of it whatsoever.

Shortly after Michalak had been cleared to leave the hospital, he was contacted by a number of people who wanted to go with him to the alleged landing site. Among these were representatives from the University of Colorado's UFO project, called the Condon Committee, and a journalist from Life Magazine.

Michalak agreed, and together they flew over Whiteshell Park in a helicopter, with the intent of locating the site from air. However, Michalak failed to do so, which according to him made the researchers doubtful of his claims, leading to them abandoning the case altogether.

Even so, later that same year he went with Canadian police and air force personnel to Whiteshell in order to find the landing site by foot. For almost an hour, they walked through heavy bush and undergrowth, over brooks, and up steep hills.

Eventually, they came upon the flat rock outcropping where Michalak said the UFO had landed. An outline of a circle, about 15 foot in diameter, could be seen on the moss and earth that was covering the rock surface. Other than that, there was no clear physical evidence that a craft had landed there.

Using radiation detectors, they found potential signs of emissions, and decided to send samples of the soil to a laboratory. As suspected, the test results revealed clear indications of radiation. To everyone's surprise, however, two different types were identified.

One was from the uranium ore which was found naturally in the area. The other source, however, was more difficult to pinpoint. It was a specific type of radiation called "radium 226", that much was clear, but where it came from was a complete mystery. When the authorities caught wind of this, they decided to temporarily close off the area of the park where the soil had been collected.

Over a year after the incident at Falcon Lake, Stephen Michalak was still feeling physically diminished. He decided to travel to the famous Mayo Clinic in Minnesota, United States, where he underwent another series of tests. After they were completed, he headed home again, thinking the clinic would contact him when the results had come in. For some unknown reason, however, they never did.

Michalak finally reached out to the Mayo Clinic and asked for his test results. To his surprise, he got sent a strange letter stating that he must have made a mistake, that he was never there, and that no tests had been performed on him whatsoever.

This apparent attempt at gaslighting did not sit well with Michalak, as he had kept both cards and medical bills from the hospital — he had no reason to doubt his own memory. Despite the denial of the Mayo Clinic, he was eventually able to get a hold of his medical records, which weirdly stated that he simply had an itchy skin disease and a transient case of sudden fainting — there was no mention of his more severe symptoms or the various tests he underwent.

In the years that followed the event at Falcon Lake, the Canadian government chose to keep a lid on the surrounding activities. When accused of a coverup, they consistently claimed that all the information about the case was documented by the National Research Council, and that everything was already available to the public.

Officially speaking, they were unable to either confirm or deny Michalak's claims of a UFO landing in the Whiteshell Provincial Park — though many independent researchers doubt this claim.

Considering the close involvement and suspicious behavior of the authorities, the sudden refusal of the Mayo Clinic to release Michalak's test results, the mysterious burns on his chest, the severe, documented physical ailments he experienced afterwards, and the odd radiation readings of the alleged landing site, it is no wonder that the Falcon Lake incident is listed among the most compelling UFO cases to date.

Chapter 7

The Mountain Of The Dead

Igor Dyatlov, a 23-year old radio engineering student, and his crew of nine friends and colleagues were expected back in the Russian town of Vizhai on February 12, 1959. Dyatlov was set to lead the group, all of whom were experienced ski-hikers, through Russia's northern Ural Mountains, which should have provided no serious problems for them.

On January 27, the group left Vizhai, which was the last town located that far north in the region, for the trek to mount Otorten (a word meaning "don't go there" in the indigenous Mansi language). One of the hikers, Yuri Yudin, turned back a day into the journey due to illness. He would be the last person to see his nine companions alive.

February 12 came and went. Yudin remained unworried; longer mountain treks often spilled over a day or two, sometimes longer, and Dyatlov had specifically told him to wait at least until the 14th before sounding any alarms. As it turned out, the 14th also passed by without any sign of the group. By February 20, Yudin and several relatives of the now-missing hikers demanded a search and rescue operation to be launched.

Police, teachers, students and local Mansi tribespeople were soon joined by military personnel, helicopters and planes. After almost a week of searching, the last campsite of Dyatlov's team was finally discovered on Kholat Syakhl — a mountain slope 6 miles south of their destination. What the search party found there left them perplexed.

The group's tent was partly torn down and covered in light snow, with almost all provisions and clothing left inside – even their shoes. Eight or nine sets of tracks leading away from the campsite indicated that some members of the group were barefoot or only wearing one shoe, despite temperatures that would have ranged between 5 and -22°F.

Puzzled, the investigators kept following the tracks. They became obscured after about 500 yards, but pointed toward a nearby woodland. At the edge of the woods, underneath a tall cedar tree, two dead bodies were found alongside the remains of a small fire.

For whatever reason, they were only partially clothed. The grisly discoveries continued, with three more bodies (including Igor Dyatlov's) being found at staggered intervals between the tree and the campsite, facing toward the tent.

Although the search went on for the remaining four missing hikers, a legal inquest began immediately. Investigators surveyed the site's geography and ruled out avalanche as a probable cause. The tent was discovered to have been cut open from the inside, and the nearby tracks suggested that the group walked, not ran, from the campsite toward the woods.

At the forest's edge, the tall cedar was found to have broken branches five meters up, possibly gathered for the fire at its base. An autopsy concluded that the five who were discovered died from hypothermia, although Rustem Slobodin (one of the three who appeared to be making their way back to the tent) also had numerous minor head wounds, including a small crack in his skull.

Over two months passed after the initial findings. The spring thaw, which the searchers hoped would clear things up, only revealed deeper mysteries. 80 yards further into the woods, at the bottom of a ravine, the final four hikers were found near a makeshift shelter on May 4th. All were wearing items of clothing belonging to other, fallen members of the group and seemed better outfitted against the cold.

The subsequent autopsy suggested that only one of the four died of hypothermia, while the other three succumbed to traumatic internal injuries, including multiple broken ribs, a heavily -fractured skull, and, in the case of one Lyudmila Dubanina, even a missing tongue. Suddenly, the head wounds found earlier in Rustem Slobodin's skull seemed much more significant.

The initial investigation by the Russian authorities concluded that the hiking group died as a result of a "compelling natural force". But what 'force', natural or otherwise, would cause nine experienced hikers to cut themselves free of their only shelter and escape into the below-freezing winter night? Why would they – some barefoot or in socks – then *walk* to the nearby woods, only for three of them to try to and make it back to camp?

To confound matters further, there are several finer details worth noting:

1. There are various claims that high levels of radiation were detected throughout the area, but comments from initial investigators only mention superficial beta-radiation — possibly from Dubanina's university lab coat.

2. At the campsite, search crews reported finding a torch *on top* of the tent. Additionally, despite the crew not having any spares with them, a ski-pole that seemed to have been intentionally cut in two was found nearby.

3. Unlike the other two members of the group which were making their way back toward camp, the ice underneath Rustem Slobodin's body had melted — indicating his body was still warm when he fell. Combined with the skull fracture, it has been suggested that he was subjected to some form of blunt force trauma on his way back to the tent.

4. Building a fire in the middle of a below-zero Russian night is not an easy task — indicating that at least some of the hikers had their wits about them.

5. Although Yuri Yudin (the surviving hiker who turned back) distinctly remembered seeing one of his fellow skiers, Alexander Kolevatov, keeping a personal diary, this item was never listed among the recovered belongings. Additionally, Yudin was later asked to identify items found at the scene, and claimed that several of them did *not* belong to any of his friends.

   These incidents (along with the military's file on the case, which supposedly dated February 6 – almost three weeks before any investigation began) led Yudin to believe that the military found the camp well before the other search crews.

The list could continue, but it gets harder to corroborate. 60 years, several deceased eye-witnesses, and the general secrecy of the Cold War-era Soviet government, has a tendency to bury things deeper than the snow. Recent articles, documentaries and Youtube videos have only confounded the matter further, repeating false information and (perhaps inadvertently) adding to the haze of myth surrounding the incident at Dyatlov Pass.

As with many unexplained mysteries of the world, it has become a sort of societal Rorscharch test – an inkblot in which we may see our deepest fears reflected. The theories have ranged from the somewhat-plausible to the ridiculous — although none are completely without flaws.

What do *you* see in the inkblot?

Theory #1: Avalanche

This theory was almost immediately ruled out by early investigators. Additionally, in the many decades since the incident took place, the hundreds of camps that have been made in the area have not been subjected to even a minor snowdrift. This does not discount the group *thinking* that an avalanche was taking place, but why would such experienced hikers then attempt a downhill escape?

Theory #2: Paradoxical Undressing

Did the hikers, in the throes of hypothermia, become delusional, undress, cut themselves from the tent, then walk off into the night? Paradoxical undressing usually occurs, if at all, in the very last stages of hypothermia. Yet the group was active for some time after leaving the tent, and were even able to make a fire in the middle of the night.

Additionally, the least-dressed hikers (found beneath the cedar) most likely died first, since items of their clothing were later found on the bodies in the ravine. Was one half of the group paradoxically undressing while the rest were sensibly dressed?

Theory #3: Ravine Fall

It has been suggested that the traumatic injuries of three of the last four hikers were from a fall into the ravine where they were found. How, then, were they able to construct a makeshift shelter at the bottom of the ravine?

Does the large amount of coagulated blood found in Lyudmila Dubanina's stomach during her autopsy support the idea of internal bleeding after a fall, or does it suggest her tongue was removed while she was still alive?

Dr Vozrojdenniy, who performed the autopsies of the hikers, described Dubanina's trauma as being equivalent to a car crash. But if the internal injuries were so pervasive, why was there no corresponding soft tissue damage?

Despite the preservative conditions of Russian winter, the last four bodies were, as mentioned, found over two months after the incident, during the spring thaw. The exact details of what occurred in that ravine, although they may be crucial to our understanding of the surrounding mystery, are perhaps the most obscured of all.

Theory #4: Cursed Mountain

Kholat Syakhl is a Mansi name meaning "mountain of the dead". Taken together with Otorten's similarly-dire meaning of "don't go there", one would naturally suspect that native people considered the area cursed.

However, the names could also refer to the scarcity of food in the area. A lack of flora and fauna meant that the Mansi, a group of hunter-gatherers, mostly avoided these areas — they simply had no use for them.

This has not stopped tales spreading of an earlier ill-fated group of Mansi hunters, or a fatal plane crash in the area (both events also apparently claiming nine lives). Though, a lack of any solid evidence seems to cast doubt on both these stories.

Theory #5: UFOs

According to several sources, there was significant UFO activity before, during, and after the incident at Dyatlov Pass. Different origins of these mysterious lights in the sky have been proposed:

extraterrestrials, interdimensionals, the military, or unexplained natural phenomena.

Lev Ivanov (a prosecutor who headed the inquest as of March, '59) went so far as to publish an article in the *Leninskyi Put* newspaper in 1990, claiming he was asked by officials to withdraw evidence of "fire balls" from his original investigation, which he believed were connected to the hikers' deaths.

Such accusations of government cover-up also bring to mind Yuri Yudin's belief that the military were at Dyatlov's campsite long before any of the other search crews.

Theory #6: Zolotarev

Conspiracy-minded folks also draw attention to Semyon 'Alexander' Zolotarev, one of the four discovered in the ravine. Zolotarev was over a decade older than the other hikers, and was not a member of the Ural Polytechnical Institute (UPI) like the others were.

In fact, he only joined Dyatlov's group at the last minute. He was initially scheduled to hike with another group, but claimed to have changed crew so that he would have time to visit his sick mother after the trip.

Kolevatov (also found in the ravine, and the former owner of the potentially-missing diary) is often drawn into the web of intrigue as well. He is said to have worked at a secret lab in Moscow prior to studying at UPI, and had plans of joining the military.

But to what ends were they supposedly working? Classified weapons testing? Did Zolotarev change hiking groups because Dyatlov's route brought him closer to some secret rendezvous, or was he just keen on seeing his mother?

Considering the amount of time that has passed, and barring the release of pertinent government documents, we are not likely to ever know what tragedy befell Igor Dyatlov and his eight companions. Each theory has its share of believers and detractors, and no one has been able to fully validate or debunk any one of them.

That being said, in a rather surprising turn of events, the Russian government officially reopened the case of the ill-fated skiers in 2019, which got the attention of international news media and paranormal researchers alike.

Some are hopeful that this will bring forth new

information, while others claim it is merely a publicity effort by the state. Whatever the case may be, as of today, what happened in Dyatlov pass during that freezing night remains a mystery.

Chapter 8

Visions Of A Killer

On February 21, 1977, Chicago firefighters entered apartment 15B on 2740 North Pine Grose Avenue and made short work of the flames they found inside. From the look of it, the fire appeared to have originated from what was now a charred mattress. Underneath it, they made a grim discovery: the body of Teresita Basa, naked and burned, with a large butcher's knife sticking out of her chest.

She was a 48-year-old Filipino respiratory therapist who had worked at the nearby Edgewater Hospital. A murder investigation was immediately opened, but the few leads the Chicago P.D. had led to dead ends. After two months, the case was declared cold and put aside. Enter Mrs. Remibias "Remy" Chua.

Like the deceased Teresita Basa, Remy and her husband José were immigrants from the Philippines. The couple also worked at Edgewater Hospital — José as a doctor, and Remy, like Teresita, as a respiratory therapist.

A fortnight after the murder, Remy had a conversation at work with the technical head of her department, Jennie Prince. Jennie said Teresita must be "turning in her grave" at the fact her killer had not been caught – *"Too bad she can't tell the police who did it",* she remarked.

Remy opened herself to the suggestion: *"She can come to me in a dream. I'm not afraid."* Later that day, while napping on a break at work, she had a feeling that something was trying to contact her. She opened her eyes and was shocked to see Teresita standing right in front of her. Remy fled the room in fear and told her colleagues what she saw.

That night, Remy dreamed of Teresita's face being shadowed by the face of a dark-skinned man. Before long, she recognized that the face belonged to Allan Showery: a 31-year-old African-American who worked as an orderly at Edgewater. She did not mention the dream to anyone at first, and began developing an aversion to Showery at work.

In July, Remy's visions reached a new level of intensity. At home one night, she dozed in and out of sleep (mirroring the state of her initial 'waking' encounter), while her husband talked on the phone to his attorney. José Chua mentioned the name "Al" and Remy screamed.

Then, seemingly in a trance, she walked to the other side of the room and laid down on the bed. *"Ako 'y Teresita Basa"* she said in Tagalog (the first language for a quarter of Filipinos) – meaning, "I am Teresita Basa". Her voice had a strange, almost Spanish-sounding accent.

She continued:

"Doctor, I would like to ask for your help. The man who murdered me is still at large."

She asked José to inform the police, but she gave no details. After a few minutes, Remy Chua finally woke up, remembering nothing. Remy, developing an increasing fear of Allan Showery, the face from her dream, left her job at Edgewater Hospital. A few weeks later, while on the phone with José, she dropped into another trance.

Speaking in Tagalog again, as Teresita Basa, Remy asked her husband if he had told the police yet. He said that he would, but he had nothing to tell them. She gave him the name "Allan", but it still was not enough to go on.

Several days later, Remy had another "Tagalog-ian" Teresita trance that gave José plenty to tell the police: her killer's name was Allan Showery, and he stole some of her jewelry to give to his girlfriend. She also mentioned the names of several people who could identify the jewelry, even providing the phone number for one of them.

Her last, chilling words were as follows:

"Tell them that Al came to fix my television, and he killed me and burned me."

José called the police and, after some initial skepticism, they went to Showery's home. The police had no warrant, but asked Showery (who was with his girlfriend at the time) to come down to the station with them. He reluctantly agreed.

When asked about the night of Basa's murder, Showery admitted that he had *arranged* to repair her television but that Basa had cancelled, so he went to work on an electrical problem back home instead. The police left Showery at the station and went to crosscheck his story with his girlfriend. That did not go down well for him, as she told them Showery did not know the first thing about fixing electrical problems.

Next, they asked if she had received any jewelry recently. She proceeded to show them the pendant and ring she was wearing — both of them given to her by Showery recently as late Christmas presents.

The police presented both pieces of jewelry to Teresita's cousin, owner of the trance-received telephone number, and she confirmed they had belonged to Teresita.

While on trial, the defense lobbied to have the case dismissed: Surely a ghost could not testify? The judge overruled, and the trial continued for a month, though the jury remained deadlocked. Eventually, a hung jury was declared.

While waiting for a retrial, Allan Showery decided to confess everything. He was sentenced to 14 years in prison for the murder of Teresita Basa, with an additional eight for aggravated arson and robbery. He would serve less than five before being released.

Although cases of possession have been recorded that appear to involve elements outside current understanding, Remy Chua seems to have undergone an explicable, albeit uncontrolled, unconscious projection.

By all accounts, she honestly believed that she was being visited by Teresita, and her husband at least believed that *she* believed it. Remy, José and Teresita were all born and raised in the Philippines – a country where folk belief, urban legend and ghost tales are both widespread and varied.

Commonly, Filipino ghosts, known as *multo*, are often thought to return in order to avenge a wrongdoing, complete a task, or correct an improper burial. They are also considered more likely to appear after a violent death or suicide.

And although it's over40 years later, it's interesting to hear that the Filipino Catholic Church said cases of demonic possession had risen "three-fold" in recent years. Chief exorcist Father José Francisco Syquia elaborated, saying *"These days, we have around 80 to 100 cases at any given time."*

It's also worth noting that the Philippines were a Spanish colony for over 300 years, until the

Americans took over in 1898 — something to think about when pondering Remy's accent while she spoke Teresitian Tagalog.

Skeptics point out that Remy worked with both victim and killer — implying she could have come across or overheard details that her subconscious mind then pieced together. And she primed her mind for the revelation with her statement: *"She can come to me in a dream. I'm not afraid"*.

Remy was dreaming when she first saw the face of the murderer revealed as Allan Showery, a state of almost pure subconscious expression. Similarly, for at least two of her possessed episodes, she was in a state of near-sleep – also known as a 'hypnopompic' state, or a period of threshold consciousness occurring between sleep and wakefulness.

Psychologists and physicians have observed an increased probability of auditory and visual hallucinations, lucid dreams, and sleep paralysis in hypnopompic subjects. In other words, Remy would have been both more in touch with her subconscious during this state, and prime to project its contents into a form she had no control over.

Another of her episodes occurred while she was on

the phone with her husband. Yet another was initiated by an overheard telephone conversation her husband was having at the time.

A telephone is an instrument of communication whereby two or more people can talk to one another without the need for physical proximity. Could this have triggered, on some level, Remy's 'communication' with someone else who was not physically present?

But now we enter the more shadowy realms of speculation. All that can be said for certain is that Teresita Basa was murdered, and her killer, Allan Showery, got let off far too lightly. As for Remibias 'Remy' Chua?

Without her, Showery could have gotten away with it entirely, been encouraged by the apparent ease, and may even have killed again. Whether Teresita's ghost was forged in the unknown recesses of a human mind or came from somewhere else entirely, it is most likely at peace now.

Chapter 9

Edgar Cayce & The Hall
Of Records

Edgar Cayce was a noted American mystic and psychic of the early 20th century who shared his visions pertaining to our ancestors, reincarnation and the future of humanity, among other things. There has since been a lot of controversy over his predictions and prophecies, their legitimacy, and what they mean for our past and, subsequently, our future.

Cayce had a preoccupation with the lost city of Atlantis, and explained the significant impact this civilization had, and will continue to have, on humanity. Cayce explained a vision he saw regarding an ancient "Hall of Records" allegedly left behind by our Atlantean ancestors.

He reported that certain Atlanteans were aware of the pending destruction of their civilization, and decided to hide three sets of records in three different locations around the world, in hopes that during the time humanity would need the information the most, we would find it. Cayce stated that these three locations were Bimini (the westernmost district of Bahamas), the Yucatan Peninsula (located in southeastern Mexico), and Egypt.

These records, he said, were inscribed on ancient tablets, and told of our shared human history. They speak of the time when spirit first took form on the land in the time of creation. They describe the developments that occurred on the land throughout this period of history, with a record of the changes that took place within the civilization, and what that lead to their ultimate annihilation.

The readings also state that there are records with information pertaining to the practice of building pyramids, in addition to linens, gold and other artifacts that complete the full story of this ancient society.

The biggest controversy lies in whether one or all of these chambers have already been discovered. Some speculate that there is active resistance amongst governments and religious groups towards finding these lost chambers, because the truth will conflict with humanity's present-day understanding of itself and its ancient history.

Considering that we have almost unlimited access to all kinds of information via the internet these days, how, exactly, would these old records be able to shock us to such a degree?

Some theories posit that this ancient civilization was so evolved that they had a deeper understanding of our true nature, whatever that may be. It could also be that there are a lot of parallels between the lost city of Atlantis and our present-day civilization. Many would argue that humanity of today sits at a crossroad: Mass enlightenment or mass destruction.

As mentioned, one place in which the records were allegedly hidden is in Egypt — not inside a tomb, or a pyramid, but underneath one of the paws of the Great Sphinx. There is some evidence that supports this assertion.

An engraving on the Dream Stele sitting between the paws of the Sphinx (mentioned in Chapter 1) shows an image of the statue itself. Underneath is what looks like a grid, with a large space far below the structure. If this drawing is to be taken literally, it could be a direct visual representation of the hidden chamber that sits beneath.

There is some evidence that points towards this being true. A radar scan around the area of one of the paws of the Sphinx showed what appears to be a chamber underneath the surface.

There is also evidence that a whole underground network of caves and tunnels snakes around the entire Giza plateau. Unfortunately, government interference has caused much difficulty in the exploration of these subterranean areas.

Seismological studies performed in 1997 by Dr. Joseph Schor and Joe Jahoda showed what looked to be an empty space beneath one of the paws, as Cayce had predicted over 60 years earlier.

The researchers stated that it had clear-cut, 90-degree angles and rectangular dimensions, which would suggest that the space was man-made. Despite this finding, however, nobody was able to explore this potential chamber due to Zahi Hawass and his crew denying anyone permits to do so.

Hawass, being the Director General of the Giza Plateau, has repeatedly slowed the process of any further exploration of the Sphinx by independent researchers. In 2001, he encouraged a hold on any excavation in the area, allegedly as to preserve the plateau and the monuments that sit on it. He also claimed that he and some colleagues had already drilled beneath the statute, but that they found nothing special except some natural cavities.

This standoffish behavior regarding the Sphinx has naturally produced much speculation, as well as whispers of conspiracy. To many people, it looks like Hawass and the Egyptian government may have reason to keep whatever is hidden beneath the Sphinx from becoming public. But if so, what could it be?

What could be so ground-breaking as to warrant such a long-lasting coverup? A Hall of Records would certainly fit the bill.

As mentioned, another possible location of the records mentioned by Cayce lies somewhere in the Yucatan Peninsula. Due to certain information in the readings, many have associated Piedras Negras as the location — an ancient Maya city in Guatemala. In the 1930's, a lot of clues lead researchers to this specific place.

Back then, an excavation by the University of Pennsylvania resulted in large piles of debris making it difficult to explore key areas. A group from the Brigham Young University (B.Y.U.), a private, non-profit research university located in Utah, United States, did years of study of this area, but the location made it difficult to perform continuous research.

It sits deep in the jungle of Guatemala, and access to the site requires days of travel through rough terrains — including traveling on white rapids and mountain roads. Since it is a rainforest, exploration is also largely limited to dry summer months, which constricts the time available for this research.

Because of this, B.Y.U. eventually moved their project and materials to a laboratory to perform further research, which slowed things down quite a bit.

The readings of Cayce say that there is a system of underground tunnels and chambers somewhere in this region, similar to those that may have been found in Egypt, which holds the ancient records. This could very well be true, since the Mayans are known to have built such underground passageways.

B.Y.U. conducted a lot of research probing the areas around the pyramids. They have confirmed that the most likely location for the Hall of Records would be around the Acropolis area. Unfortunately, many of the ruins that lay there are considered unstable, as their foundations are thought to have been built around 400-600 BC.

This makes it difficult and risky to perform any large-scale digs there. Nevertheless, according to the prophecy from Cayce and the evidence that has been found in the excavations thus far, this sounds like the most reasonable place to look.

The third and final location of the Hall of Records is supposed to be somewhere near the Bimini Islands off the coast of the Bahamas. Edgar Cayce stated that the tablets could be found in a temple that is currently submerged, but which he said "will rise, and is rising again." According to legend, this temple was that of a man called Atlan — a high priest of Atlantis who preserved the records here.

In 1968, near the Bimini Islands, the so-called Bimini Road was discovered — an underwater rock formation mostly made up of rectangular limestone blocks.

According to Cayce, Bimini was very close in location to the largest island occupied by Atlanteans that was destroyed around 10.000 BC. Some researchers have posited that the Bimini Road was one of the main routes between the Atlantean settlements that used to exist in the region.

Photographic surveys of the nearby area have shown evidence of a possible submerged city. Some of these formations appear to be shaped like pentagons and pyramids, and seem to be part of old buildings (or what's left of them).

Skeptics have stated that there is always the possibility of old shipwrecks being misinterpreted as something else. However, in 1977, the independent researcher Dr. Joan Hanley closely examined the area and argued that the formation was most likely intelligently made, due to so many different stones laying side-by-side each other in such an orderly fashion.

Further research of the underwater area was conducted in the 1990's, which provided more evidence of a submerged city. A formation similar to the Bimini Road was found, this time south of Bimini.

A search that was named Project Alta in 1993 reported evidence of a wide hexagonal formation on the ocean floor, along with other unnatural formations such as concentric circles, triangular shapes and right angles that appeared most unusual. Since then, various individuals and organizations have conducted sonar research, but the results remain inconclusive.

The predictions of Edgar Cayce still echo to this day, speaking of the potential of making ground-breaking discoveries about our past. Some believe that the information that was allegedly hidden long ago by our Atlantean ancestors will reveal itself at the right time.

We have yet to obtain substantive evidence of the existence of the three chambers. However, all of the clues that we currently hold certainly seem to point towards them being real.

Some say that the Hall of Records is a metaphor for the knowledge that was lost from the civilizations that came before us. Others refer to them as a symbol of the so-called Akashic Records — a library of infinite thoughts, emotions and wisdom that can be accessed in a non-physical plane of existence.

If Atlantis truly existed and somehow fell from grace, it is certainly in our best interest to use whatever we can find to restore the ancient wisdom they held onto.

Maybe this information will come from a chamber hidden deep in the sea, maybe it will be found deep underground beneath a sacred temple. Or, perhaps it will be found in our very own collective remembering of a better way of living.

Whatever the case may be, the hunt for the Hall of Records is far from over. With more and more passionate seekers joining in on the search, who knows what the future will bring?

Chapter 10

Ghost Lights

If you tell someone that you have seen a mysterious light in the night, chances are they will think of a UFO — an object of some sort that is giving off a strong glow while hovering high in the sky. And that is definitely the most common report when it comes to such paranormal phenomena. However, there is another, closely related anomaly which is often overlooked: ghost lights.

While UFOs are usually large and airborne, ghost lights are smaller and appear near the ground. This gives them a more spiritual or ghostly feeling rather than extraterrestrial, hence the name. Interestingly, ghost lights have been witnessed all over the world throughout history.

They are mostly spotted in deep forests, around or above marshes, and in graveyards. Though the theories of their true nature vary from country to country, their general description stays more or less the same: medium-sized balls of light which seem to have, or are controlled by, some sort of intelligence.

They usually hover in place, just above ground level. However, they have been known to recede when people try to approach them, and sometimes follow those who walk away.

They feature most prominently in British folklore, where they are best known as "will-o'-the-wisp" — a name which many fantasy enthusiasts will also recognize, as they can be found in several popular fictional works. Other names given to these mysterious orbs are "Jack-o'-lantern" (which gave rise to the famous Halloween decoration), "Jenny with the lantern", and "Peg-a'-lantern", among many, many others.

These names reflect the old popular belief that the lights were actually lanterns being carried around by mischievous, shapeshifting spirits. They would make them glow brightly during the night in order to lure someone deep into the woods.

Then, they would blow out the light and take pleasure in watching the person fumbling through the darkness in fear. On some occasions, however, they have been said to show benevolent qualities — when seemingly guiding lost children back to their homes, for example.

On the other side of the planet, in Asia, there have also been plenty of ghost light sightings throughout the centuries. The Bengali people call them "Aleya", which are said to be spirits of deceased fishermen that hover over marshes and bodies of water. In Japan, they are called "Hitodama" — believed to be human souls appearing as balls of pure energy. Further down south, in Australia, they are referred to as Min Min lights, which are known to follow travelers for long distances.

In the United States, ghost lights, also known as spook lights, have been reported in several rural areas. One of the places with the most frequent sightings is near Marfa, Texas — an isolated small town of about 2000 inhabitants.

The first documented mention of the so-called "Marfa lights" go all the way back to 1883, when a ranch helper named Robert Ellison spotted them one late evening while herding cattle. He was told by the early settlers of the area that they had observed the lights for many years. When they tried to approach and investigate them, they would always disappear without a single trace.

As the years went by, more and more people started seeing the ghost lights of Marfa, and soon they garnered national attention. Paranormal researchers, skeptics and curious tourists all came to get a glimpse of the mysterious orbs.

Eventually, the continued influx of light-seeking travelers prompted locals to create businesses and tourist attractions related to the phenomenon. They made t-shirts, mugs, a delegated viewing area marked by a large sign, and even an annual event called "The Marfa Lights Festival". Most travelers never get a chance to see the enigmatic lights, though, as even a hotspot will only yield the occasional sighting.

Those who have been lucky enough to see them in action report the usual will-o'-the-wisp description: Luminous orbs around the size of basketballs, hovering to and from, appearing and disappearing, and sometimes even splitting into two equally-sized spheres.

Their colors vary from light green or pure white to dark orange or red. Onlookers can enjoy the light show for quite some time at a distance. However, as usual, when they try to get close to the glowing spheres, they either vanish or move farther away — leaving behind no physical evidence.

Many skeptics have tried to explain away the phenomenon by attributing it to various natural processes. One of the most cited explanations is one which UFO researchers know all too well: swamp gas. It is said that the ghost lights are caused by the oxidation of methane, phosphine, and diphosphane — natural compounds which are produced by decaying matter in marshes and swamps. This is generally accepted by the mainstream science community since a large share of ghost light sightings take place near such areas.

Still, this theory leaves a lot to be desired. For one, this does not explain how the orbs have been seen hovering steadily over the ground with a constant light intensity. The fact that ghost lights are known to move away from the marshes and other "gassy" areas where they first appeared also throws a wrench in this theory.

Furthermore, in countries such as the United States and Australia, the luminous spheres emerge in the middle of deserts and mountainous landscapes, but still have more or less the same appearance as the ones found in the wet forests of Europe.

A number of scientists and debunking enthusiasts have tried to create their own ghost lights, in order to disprove the paranormal nature of the phenomenon. In 1980, for example, a British geologist by the name of Alan Mills tried to create a will-o'-the-wisp inside a laboratory using natural gas and phosphine.

After many attempts, he finally had to admit defeat. He only managed to make a momentary effect of a greenish light that was followed by a pocket of hot air and, most importantly, a large cloud of smoke, which is not reported in ghost light encounters.

Another attempt at debunking the phenomenon, specifically the Marfa lights, was made by a group of physics students from the University of Texas at Dallas. Their theory was that car lights from the nearby U.S. Highway 67 were shining towards the viewing area and appeared to be ghost lights in the dark.

After 4 days spent studying the location and nearby

traffic, they decided that all the Marfa lights sightings could simply be attributed to cars from the nearby highway.

While many accepted this conclusion, others found it lacking, noting that the car lights are far too dim and indistinct compared to the bright-lit spheres that people have come to know.

Also, the theory failed to account for the wide range of spectacular movements that the ghost lights have been observed performing — sometimes they are completely stationary, sometimes they dart around the desert at incredible speed, while other times they can be seen bobbing back and forth in an almost-rhythmic fashion.

The previously-mentioned tendency to move further away when people try to get close to them is not sufficiently explained by the car lights theory, either.

A retired NASA aerospace engineer who grew up around Marfa, James Bunnell, returned to the area in the year of 2000 and witnessed what he described as a shocking light display which had no reasonable explanation.

Moved by the awe-inspiring sight, he spent almost 12 years investigating the local ghost lights afterwards. With permission from his neighbors, he installed 10 infrared cameras in the surrounding area in order to film them from several angles.

As he looked through the footage, he was searching for a discernable pattern in their movement or time of appearance. However, after sorting through every single recording, he failed to do so.

Bunnell has a few theories about the true nature of the Marfa lights — one involving electromagnetic activity due to underground friction. Still, after over a decade of research, the phenomenon remains an enigma.

Whatever the true nature of these mysterious lights, they are still being seen around the world today. If you find yourself in a forest or remote desert at night, look out for an apparent bright flashlight in the distance. If you fail to spot someone holding it, you may very well have come across the elusive will-o'-the-wisp.

Chapter 11

The Answer From Elsewhere

In May of 1899, Nikola Tesla, mad genius extraordinaire, moved to a Colorado Springs experimental station in order to develop and test theories relating to radio transmission, electric fields and resonant frequencies.

He would soon prove to live up to his eccentric reputation. His stay was accompanied by artificial lightning, light-bulb filaments that would not shut off, arcing sparks beneath the feet of passing pedestrians, butterflies haloed by St Elmo's fire, and a sudden power station outage. Suffice to say, it was an interesting nine months.

Apart from detecting stationary waves and the resonant frequency of the earth, Tesla also claimed to have witnessed something far stranger, as he stated:

"The feeling is constantly growing on me that I had been the first to hear the greeting of one planet to another."

He had noted an unknown signal that changed periodically — one which, to his mind, was not accidental. What was it? A mistake, or something more?

In the same article ('Talking With Planets'), Tesla went on to say:

"I can readily demonstrate that, with an expenditure not exceeding two thousand horsepower, signals can be transmitted to a planet such as Mars with as much exactness and certitude as we now send messages by wire from New York to Philadelphia."

75 years later, a team of scientists would broadcast the first such intentional message toward a globular star cluster known to astronomers as M13.

The message (written by Frank Drake and Carl Sagan, among other contributors) was sent from the Arecibo radio telescope in Puerto Rico — an observatory that dwarfs Nikola Tesla's 280-foot experimental tower. The 1000-foot wide collecting dish is the largest in the world, having been constructed inside the remains of a giant karst sinkhole.

Re-modelling was completed in 1974 and, to demonstrate the power of the new dish, a message was broadcast to a star cluster 25,000 light years away. The less-than-three-minute radio message was a mere 210 bytes.

Arranged graphically, top to bottom, the binary digits conveyed the following seven pieces of information:

1. The numbers one to ten.

2. The atomic numbers of the elements that form DNA.

3. Nucleotide formulas (the constituents of DNA).

4. The image of a DNA double helix, including nucleotide pairs.

5. The image of a human, including average height and global population.

6. The solar system, with the third planet highlighted (and Pluto still included).

7. An image of the Arecibo dish the message was sent from, along with its proportions.

Although it would take a long time for the message to reach M13 (the broadcast was more a show of capability rather than a serious communication attempt), scientists *did* detect a strange signal less than three years later, originating from a different globular star cluster – M55.

Known as the 'Wow! signal' (named after a margin-scribbled 'Wow!' on the computer printout), it lasted the full 72 seconds that Ohio's 'Big Ear' telescope was pointed at it. It was never repeated, and remains unexplained to this day.

27 years after the Arecibo "message-in-a-bottle" was sent, a field near the Chilbolton Observatory in the English county of Hampshire received a reply — a direct one at that. A crop circle (well, rectangle) appeared, apparently overnight, in August, 2001. Amazingly, it bore an uncanny resemblance to the original Arecibo broadcast.

This apparent response mirrored the seven items of information contained in the original message, with some notable differences.

They were as follows:

1. The numbering system is also based 1 to 10.

2. Silicon is present along with the standard DNA elements.

3. The constituents of nucleotides are the same.

4. The DNA has an extra helix and extra pairs of nucleotides.

5. An image of what looks like a classic 'grey'

alien is shown, with an indicated height of 3'4 and global population of 12.7 billion.

6. Nine planets are depicted. However, the sun is smaller and planets 3, 4 and 5 are highlighted — seemingly indicating habitation.

7. A circular object with appendages, which actually appeared separately in another crop circle *in the same field* a year before, is depicted as the communication device.

A year after this mind-boggling formation, yet another incredible crop circle in yet another Hampshire field containing yet another code was discovered. It showed what looked like a detailed portrait of an extraterrestrial being similar to the classical grey type, but with visible pupils and a longer face.

It looked to be holding a type of disc with a bunch of markings in it, which later turned out to contain a binary code comprised of no less than 1368 ones and zeros.

When a computer expert managed to decode it, he

found a cohesive message embedded in the round shape. Also linked by many to the Chilbolton response, it read as follows:

"Beware the bearers of false gifts & their broken promises. Much pain but still time. Believe. There is good out there. We oppose deception. Conduit closing. (Bell sound)."

Despite its huge size and highly-detailed contents, the Chilbolton response is considered by many to be a hoax. However, the fact that no one in the area managed catch even a single glimpse of any suspicious human activity seems quite strange, especially considering the incredible intricacy and vast scope of the imprints.

Since nobody ever saw or heard anyone or anything the nights that the impressive crop circles emerged, none can say for sure who the makers really are. And so, the mystery remains.

Chapter 12

Stonehenge & Superhenge

Beneath a tourist car park in Wiltshire, England, lie the earliest signs of human activity near the world-famous Stonehenge – a handful of 10,000-year-old 'postholes', originally holding thick pine posts arranged east-west.

The people who left them are all but forgotten, and there is precious little contextual understanding of what led their descendants to erect Britain's most famous monument. Unfortunately, as the singer Joni Mitchell lamented, someone paved paradise and put up a parking lot.

Similarly, whatever lay buried in the center of Stonehenge will likely never be known thanks to the efforts of amateur 'barrow-diggers'. In 1839, one Captain Beamish carelessly dug out 400 cubic feet of earth from inside the circle, destroying whatever laid buried there.

Still, there are other prenatal precursors in the area as well. A causeway enclosure was constructed at Robin Hood's Ball around 4,000 BCE, and evidence from the nearby Blick settlement indicates that the area was in use the following millennium, resulting in structures that are only now being uncovered.

Then, around 3500 BCE, the 'Stonehenge Cursus'

was built. Originally thought to be Roman race tracks, the cursuses of Neolithic Britain (numbering at least 50) served a purpose we still do not understand. The Stonehenge Cursus has an additional interesting feature: Two artificial pits dug on the east and west ends that align with both the rising and setting of the sun at summer solstice.

This not only strengthens the theory that the cursuses had ritual significance (perhaps tracing solar cycles), but also suggests that Stonehenge should be viewed in connection with its surroundings. 'Woodhenge', for example, was built around the same time as it's stony sibling, and seems to have been used in conjunction with it. But for what, exactly? That is the question.

By 3,100 BCE, a chalk bank and ditch enclosure circled by 56 pits dominated the site. As with the Stonehenge Cursus, it's unknown what the Aubrey holes were used for. Theories have included wooden post-holders, astronomical devices, or even the original holes for standing bluestones (which would mean megalithic construction began at Stonehenge 500 years earlier than currently thought).

In 2013, the remains of 63 cremated skeletons dating from this era of construction were unearthed, adding to finds in the surrounding area that indicate that the site at least partially functioned as a graveyard.

Remains at nearby Durrington Walls, believed by some to be an early Stonehenge builders camp, show people came from far and wide to the area. Animal bones indicate gatherings of roughly 4,000 people around the solstices, which would be a true feat for the dispersed populations of Neolithic Britain.

2600 - 2400 BCE marked the beginnings of megalithic construction at the site. This is when the monument we know today started taking shape. It began with a bluestone circle (oriented precisely toward midwinter sunset / midsummer sunrise), which was soon after knocked down and encircled by 30 huge sarsen stones weighing 25 tons each.

These were topped by an additional 30 stone lintels attached using mortise and tenon style joints. The bluestones were then again incorporated as an inner ring. It was, and still is, an awe-inspiring construction. But who were the people who built it, and how did they accomplish it?

There are even older stone circles found around the world as well: The previously-mentioned Göbekli Tepe in Turkey, the sunken Atlit Yam off the coast of Israel, Nabta Playa in the Southern Egyptian deserts, the Portuguese Almendres Cromlech complex, Malta's Xaghra Circle and the Zorats Karer in Armenia, all of which pre-date Stonehenge – some by more than 5,000 years. Did stone-circle-building come naturally to the Brits, or did they draw inspiration from someone else?

Although history gets decidedly murky before the written word emerged, there was at least one significant cultural movement going on in Europe that would make its way to the British Isles, and it happened at the same time Stonehenge became megalithic. Not much is known about these so-called Beaker people. Their geographic origins, migratory movements, colonial impact, and even classification as a culture have been widely contested.

Named after their distinctive style of pottery, they have become associated with the spread of Bronze Age ideas throughout western Europe — indeed, they are thought to have brought metalworking, alcohol, woven garments, and even patriarchal society into Britain.

Earlier Neolithic cultures were typically more communal and egalitarian, but Beaker culture brought the idea of the ruling warrior-king. Long-barrow graves, mass tombs for the undifferentiated dead, became replaced with barrow mounds (or *tumuli*) — individual graves adorned with status-signifying goods. The Bronze Age was here, and one of the people who brought it with him was a man the press dubbed 'the King of Stonehenge'.

In May 2002, excavations began in Amesbury for a new school three miles from Stonehenge. Work was soon stopped when the remains of a 4300-year-old gravesite were unearthed — roughly contemporary with construction of Stonehenge's first megaliths.

"The Amesbury Archer", as he became known, was buried along with the largest amount of artifacts found in any Bronze Age British grave, including two gold hair tresses – the first securely dated gold in all of Britain.

Perhaps the most interesting part, study of the Archer's Bell-Beaker-style pottery, arrowheads, and tooth enamel, revealed that he came from the European Alps — probably Switzerland or Germany. Why did he come so far? Did he know of Stonehenge? A royal metalworker, perhaps Britain's first, bringing revolutionary ideas and materials to a Neolithic culture... did he inaugurate the first set of bluestone circles?

At some point during his youth, the Amesbury Archer sustained a traumatic leg injury, leaving him with a bone infection and a lifelong limp. He also had a tooth abscess that penetrated his jaw, begging the question as to why he made the journey in the first place. Did he limp all the way, or was he carried across Europe?

Professors Darvill and Wainwright have noted that around half of the bodies found at Stonehenge were from outside the area, and an "abnormal number" of skeletons show serious signs of disease and injury. According to their theory, Stonehenge was renowned across the European mainland as a center of healing.

If this were so, it would certainly give motivation for the Archer's pilgrimage. What effect did this copper-and-gold-working Bronze Age magician have on Neolithic culture? Did he bring stone circle secrets from further beyond? Ultimately, his secrets may have been buried forever with him. But with the rate of new archaeological discoveries and timeline rewrites, the answers, and yet more questions, may well be waiting underground.

In 2014, some of these questions came to the forefront when archaeologist Vince Gaffney, in conjunction with the Stonehenge Hidden Landscapes Project, published the results of an extensive underground survey of Stonehenge and the surrounding area.

It showed that at least 15 previously unknown Neolithic constructions laid underneath. Also discovered was the artificial 'pit' on the east side of the Cursus, showing a solstice alignment with Stonehenge's 'Heel Stone'. Gaffney believes these correlations extended further, amounting to a kind of processional route through the sacred area.

Archaeologists Mike Parker Pearson and Ramilisonina have expressed similar opinions. Based on their findings, they believe that a funerary procession beginning at Woodhenge in the east proceeded down the Avon and terminated at Stonehenge — mirroring proposed ideologies of birth (wood), the course of life (river), and death (stone).

Could Stonehenge, its Cursus, the Avon River and Woodhenge have composed a greater whole, a sort of sacred landscape? Further evidence was uncovered, or detected, by the Stonehenge Hidden Landscapes Project in September of 2015.

The nearby Durrington Walls, believed to have originally been a builder's camp for Stonehenge workers, revealed a previously-unknown circle of what looked to be 90 huge stones buried beneath the banked enclosure. Measuring 1640 feet in diameter, archaeologists dubbed it "Superhenge". They speculated that it comprised a megalithic circle roughly contemporary with Woodhenge, Stonehenge and the Cursus.

When this supposed Superhenge was finally excavated, however, everyone was met with quite a surprise — there were no giant stones to be found. Instead, the area was filled with lots of circular pits that were dug five feet deep.

The researchers believed that they were once used to anchor a number of huge, wooden poles, which together created a large monument. They speculated that it was being raised around 4500 years ago, with the intent of paying tribute to the original builders of Stonehenge.

However, the humongous timber monument was never finished, as the people who worked on it suddenly abandoned it for some reason and moved on from the area.

Shortly after, someone apparently dislodged all the timber before filling the holes with chalk. Strangely enough, there were no signs of the giant poles being rocked back and forth or pulled from the side — they had been lifted straight out of the ground in smooth, vertical motions.

If the findings of the ground-penetrating radar were correct, the giant wooden monument may have used over 300 trees. This baffled the researchers, as dense forests were not thought to have existed in this area at the time of its construction.

As is the case with Stonehenge, how the builders of the massive timber ring acquired the heavy resources, and how they managed to transport them all the way to the construction site, remains shrouded in the past — at least for now.

Chapter 13

Murder Clues From Beyond

On a cold February night in 1983, Jaqueline Poole, a 25-year-old barmaid from Ruislip, London, went completely silent. No friends, colleagues, or family members could get a hold of her on the phone, and none of her neighbors had seen her leave her apartment. When Jaqueline's father came to check up on her the next day, he was met with a locked door. No matter how hard he knocked or how loud he shouted, no movement could be heard inside.

Distressed, the father went to the backside of the building and managed to get inside through one of the half-open windows. To his horror, in the middle of the living room he found his daughter lifeless on the floor. Physical examinations would later reveal that she had been savagely beaten, raped and strangled to death.

The following Monday morning, a woman named Christine Holohan heard the news about the murder, and kept it in her mind throughout the day — feeling sorry for the victim and worrying about the killer being on the loose.

Later, as she was about to go to sleep, she suddenly started getting visions of a young woman who went by the name of Jacqui Hunt. This was later revealed to be the family name of Jaqueline Poole.

Though a bit shook by the incident, Holohan was no stranger to psychic visions and other paranormal phenomena, as she had experienced them repeatedly throughout her life.

The next day, she went about her usual business. Later in the evening, however, things would once again start to get weird, as she was allegedly visited by a spirit which manifested itself as a bright, white light with a faint outline of a human being.

This spirit, Holohan said, told her about the Poole murder in extensive detail, which made her believe it was actually the murdered woman herself. Or, more specifically, the spirit which had experienced life on Earth as Jaqueline Poole. According to Holohan, the spirit told her that Jaqueline Poole was supposed to be at work the night she was murdered, but decided to stay home due to an illness.

Out of nowhere, a familiar but unpleasant man knocked on her door. Poole, thinking that he came with news from her boyfriend, chose to let him inside her apartment. This would prove to be a grave mistake, as within minutes the man attacked her in the bathroom — beating her repeatedly until she could not resist anymore. Then, he proceeded to brutally rape her, before finally strangling her to death on the floor.

After being showered with information about the recent murder, Christine Holohan decided to contact the local police station to offer assistance to the investigation.

She was allowed to meet with officer Tony Batters and detective Andrew Smith, who were both skeptical when they heard about her supposed psychic visions. Nevertheless, Holohan managed to convince them to at least hear her out. She did this by relaying very personal and detailed information about Andrew Smith, which startled the two men.

In total, Christine Holohan gave the officials over 130 separate notes about the case — many of which were extremely precise in nature. The investigation of the murder scene eventually showed that, astoundingly enough, Holohan's explanation of the event was correct. Though Jaqueline Poole's body was located in the living room, the forensics indicated that the attack started in the bathroom, just as she had stated.

Furthermore, a slew of minor details, such as how many cups were left out in the kitchen, which furniture had been moved during the attack, the exact clothing Poole was wearing that day etc., were also checked off the list. This impressed the investigators, who then decided they would continue working with the apparent psychic.

Holohan also let the officers know about Jaqueline Poole's past involvement with criminal gangs, as well as her struggles with clinical depression. These very personal details were later confirmed by a close friend of the murdered woman. Surprisingly, she also correctly named a close friend of Jaqueline Poole who died over two years before the killing, in addition to Poole's boyfriend, brother, mother, best friend, and even the mother of her boyfriend.

Concerning the killer, Holohan stated that he was an acquaintance of Poole's ex-husband. In one of the meetings with the officials, the psychic seemed to be channeling information from somewhere else when she stated:

"The link is with nick. Both had the same friend who was in nick. Not nick, she says, 'bird.' She went to visit him two weeks before, in the bird."

"Nick" is common British slang for prison, while "bird", in this case, means detention center. Holohan did not know the difference between these terms, and was quite confused when she relayed the information to the officers. Interestingly, however, Jaqueline Poole was well aware of these slang words, due to her past involvement with criminals.

Soon after the claim of the prison visit was made, the police contacted the staff who worked there, who then confirmed that it was true. Just like Holohan stated, Poole had met with her ex-husband just two weeks prior to the murder. The psychic also received very detailed information about the killer himself.

She described him as follows:

"Five foot eigthish, dark skin, Afro-wavy hair, early 20's. She knows him. April-May date of birth. He is Taurus. Tattoos on his arms. Swords. Snake. Rose. I get a name... Tony. Goes by a nickname, not his proper name."

Furthermore, it was mentioned that this man, Tony, had been doing painting work for quick cash. He did not have a regular, stable job, had robbed several houses, and was skilled when it came to cars — both as a thief and a mechanic.

The authorities questioned Holohan about Tony's nickname, which prompted her to close her eyes and apparently enter some sort of trance state. She then grabbed a pen and paper while her eyes were still closed, and slowly wrote down the name "pokie".

As it turned out, the man who ended up being arrested, an astounding 18 years after committing the murder, was one Anthony Ruark — a 5'9 mixed-race man who was born in late April (the star sign of Taurus) and was covered in tattoos.

He was 23 years of age when he carried out the rape and murder of Jaqueline Poole. The information about his criminal activity and lack of job prospects was also true, along with his skills pertaining to the theft and repair of cars, as well as his special nickname, Pokie.

The reason it took so long for the police to arrest him was that, despite the overwhelming amount of information Holohan gave them, there was no solid evidence which could convict him of the murder. It was not until new technology became available that they were able to study the physical clues in greater detail.

Forensic experts examined the old evidence with an extremely precise technique named "DNA low profile number testing", and found genetic traces of Jacqueline Poole on a sweater they recovered from Ruark's trash. Furthermore, they found small pieces of his skin under the nails of the victim, which most likely got lodged there when she desperately tried to fight him off.

Anthony Ruark, who thought he had gotten away with the brutal rape and murder, was obviously surprised to be faced with the charges 18 years after the fact.

He failed in trying to defend himself from the allegations, first stating that he was at a pub the night of the event, but then suddenly changing his story, claiming he had consensual sex with Poole before leaving her apartment while she was still alive. In the end, the jury found him guilty, and Judge Kenneth Machin stated he had been convicted due to overwhelming evidence.

While Christine Holohan's psychic insights could not be directly used to convict Anthony Ruark, they were proven to be correct almost two decades later.

Considering the staggering number of details she gave about Jaqueline Poole's murder, this case may very well be a real example of psychic powers in action.

Chapter 14

The Men in Black

Case #1: See You Later

The date was September 3, 1965. Two Texan sheriffs, Deputy Bob Goode and Chief Deputy Bill McCoy were on patrol. Goode, nursing an alligator bite from earlier that night, drove down Highway 36 with McCoy riding shotgun. It was almost 11PM when, on the horizon, they both saw a strange light in the clear night sky.

They debated for a few minutes about what it was before pulling over to get a better look. It was purple, with a blue light that seemed to move slowly within it. They drove closer and stopped again to watch — Goode resting his wounded hand out the open window.

Suddenly, and with great speed, the light began moving towards the car. It stopped 150 feet away in a nearby pasture, about 100 feet off the ground. Strangely, the long grass underneath it remained undisturbed. Both sheriffs agreed that the object was triangular-shaped, grey, 200 feet wide, 40-50 feet tall, and made no noise.

The grass, highway, and car interior were all illuminated by the predominantly-purple glow. Goode, the closer of the two, felt a faint heat emanating from the unknown object. After a few moments, fear seized them and they took off down the highway, reaching speeds of 110mph. McCoy kept watch out the back, half-expecting it to follow them. Instead, it "snapped back" to its original position over the horizon.

The panic subsided and the sheriffs went back to investigate further. The object did the same thing, and this time the men took off and did not turn back. As the car returned to a regular speed, McCoy noticed that Goode was using his left hand again.

He remarked:

"Well, Bob, the only good thing about this is, it's made you forget about your finger."

Goode was startled. Indeed, his left hand was on the steering wheel. He pulled over and unwrapped the bandage. Not only had the alligator bite stopped bleeding, but there was no redness or swelling — it had somehow healed.

Goode threw the bandage away and the pair made a beeline for Jim Scott, City Judge of West Columbia. Judge Scott went out there with them, waiting an hour for the light to reappear, but nothing could be seen.

Several days later, but before local press had gotten wind of the story, the sheriff's station dispatch received a telephone call. Someone wanted to speak to McCoy about the UFO sighting he had recently had. They were informed that he was not in town but that Deputy Goode was at lunch nearby.

Two men, claiming to be reporters from a publication called Pasadena, found Goode at a local restaurant. Before he could tell them anything, however, they launched into a detailed description of what he had seen.

Baffled, he listened as they went on to tell him that if the sheriffs had not fled, the object would have landed and they would have been greeted by beings much like themselves, taken aboard, and then returned upon promise of silence.

The two men then left the stunned sheriff in the restaurant, never bothering to come back to speak to McCoy. The following Monday, McCoy returned, heard the news, and began inquiries at different 'Pasadenas' in several nearby states. But no one knew of the mysterious reporters, who were never seen again after the incident.

Ellington Air Force Base's Major Leach headed an

investigation into the bizarre affair – it would be one of 1600 cases that the infamous Project Blue Book (the official United States Airforce UFO study) listed as 'unidentified'.

In his conclusion, Leach stated:

"There is no doubt in my mind that they definitely saw some unusual object or phenomenon...

Both officers appeared to be intelligent, mature, level-headed persons capable of sound judgement and reasoning."

Case #2: Late-Night Bender

It was September 16, 1953. Albert Bender, director of the recently-formed International Flying Saucer Bureau, arrived home from a two-week vacation. He entered his room to find a sulfur-like smell and the white noise of a radio he had not left on. He opened the windows, switched off the radio, and went downstairs for a snack.

It was late, so after brushing his teeth, he returned to his room to prepare for sleep. Suddenly, blue lights appeared from nowhere and flew around him. Bender felt dizzy and stumbled to the bed. After laying there for some time, he suddenly became aware of three figures around him, floating a foot above the floor.

All of them seemed to be dressed in black suits, and wore hats similar to the homburg style. Their faces were obscured, but despite the circumstances, Bender felt fear leave and a light feeling wash over him. The visitors' eyes lit up "like flashlight bulbs" before they communicated with him mentally, asking him to refer to them simply as 1, 2 and 3.

They told him of various plans they had for earth and for him, before giving him a shiny piece of metal and a simple instruction: If he wanted to contact them again, he had to turn his radio on, hold the metal object in his hands, and repeat the word "Kazik" out loud. The three black-suited strangers then disappeared.

As bizarre as the encounter was, Bender went on to describe the entities to his colleagues. He initially kept details of their mission a secret, so the account published in the October '53 edition of the IFSB's *Space Review* was low on the detail, high on mystery.

Who were these three shadow men? Did they threaten Bender not to reveal certain saucer secrets? Unknowingly, Bender's moderately-successful *Space Review* publication helped launch a new UFOlogical phenomena – the Men in Black.

The sheriff and Bender cases exemplify the diversity of the Men in Black (or MIB) phenomenon – rarely will two stories sound the same. Nevertheless, if you generalize the MIB reports into a single narrative, you end up with the following 6 commonalities:

1. The experience occurs shortly after a UFO sighting, but before the witness has told anyone.

2. While the witness is home alone, a sudden loud knock is heard at the door. The visitors are three men, extremely pale yet vaguely oriental in appearance, with markedly stiff and awkward movement.

3. They wear black suits, ties, shoes, and hats with white shirts – everything appears brand-new, but is being worn somewhat uncomfortably.

4. The men possess detailed knowledge of the UFO sighting in question. They flash a badge and, speaking in stilted, mechanical tones, claim to be from a government agency. They threaten the witness to keep quiet about the UFO, sometimes using phrases like those used by 'tough guys' in '40's gangster films.

5. After a final warning, they walk out to the driveway and leave in a large black Cadillac. The car is an old model, but appears immaculate. The number plates, if recorded, are later found to be non-existent.

6. Excluding the last decade (and the online trend of faux-articles and "creepypastas"), almost half of all MIB reports come from 1966 - 1968, and almost all of *those* come from America. Although experienced worldwide, U.S. encounters dominate the literature. Why is that? And why the bizarre behavior? Let us start with "the collective subconscious".

Carl Jung had a theory: beneath every personal subconscious swims a shared, 'collective' subconscious, teeming with primal human forces. To him (and to many who followed) this belief was supported by reoccurring motifs in both dream and mythological narratives, motifs he called 'archetypes'.

Of particular interest is the archetype known as the Trickster, which falls under the broader Jungian concept of the Shadow (more on that shortly). Tricksters, like Men in Black, manifest in variations of a basic form. One instant they are malicious pranksters (they rarely follow through on threats), the next, almost savior-like figures (several encounters resemble divine disclosures, *à la* Bender's).

Jung connected Trickster expression to poltergeist phenomena and other elements of parapsychology. This, too, mirrors the tendency MIB case reports have of including other 'fringe topics' like cryptozoology or time-travel.

And the Shadow? Put simply, it is the dark spot cast by the light of the Ego. An individual's Shadow personifies their fears, anxieties, and repressions. Could the MIB be Shadow-selves of modern society, molded in our collective unconscious?

Consider the following:

- Although Tricksters traditionally manifest alone, typically-modern insecurities involve bureaucracy, red-tape, and governmental control. All have grown exponentially since WWII, and all are reflected time and again in American culture. It is worth noting that the first, sketchy version of Bender's encounter came out in '53 — in the middle of a wave of McCarthy-era fears.

Variations on MIB attire also illustrate the aforementioned insecurities. Reports often describe CIA spooks, tax men, journalists, Air Force personnel, undertakers, and insurance salesmen.

- Like an intruding subconscious thought, the MIB do not quite 'fit' with their surroundings. Their manner of speech and movement, stilted, surreal, and nonsensical, resembles a dream intruding on rational waking life — with no regard for common laws of space and time. Their items (cars, clothes, watches) are simultaneously fresh-looking and old-fashioned.

- Furthermore, the witness often enters a trance-like state before or during the encounter, making them ideally receptive to either conscious or subconscious suggestion.

As the sheriff's story shows, however, the annals of

the paranormal are dotted with cases that seem to have an observable physical element — they happened, to some extent at least, within the bounds of consensus reality.

Could this argue for a *Tulpa*-like force, which allows projections from our collective unconscious to physically enter our world (also known as thought-forms)? Or is there something even stranger going on?

Whatever the true nature of the Men in Black, they have certainly left a lasting impact on the field of UFOlogy. Though less frequent than during the 60's, encounters are still being reported to this day.

Conclusion

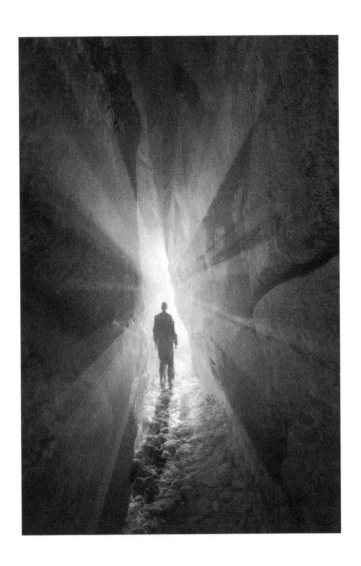

We have now gone through a wide array of baffling mysteries from all over the world. While some may be more esoteric than others, none can deny that they are all very, very interesting.

Using our precious time to ponder or even investigate such enigmas may seem like a waste to some people. However, it is important to remember that some of the greatest discoveries of humanity's history happened due to pursuing the mysterious.

As a famous theoretical physicist once said:

"The most beautiful thing we can experience is the mysterious. It is the source of all true art and science."

In our modern worldview, we tend to scoff at a perceived superstitious past full of blind spots that we have now supposedly left behind. We often like to think that we have most of it dialed in, and that there are few mysteries left.

Nevertheless, those who truly pay attention will know that the more answers we find, the more questions seem to arise. It is truly a fascinating reality we find ourselves in.

While it is certainly good to be grounded within the known, it is also worth contemplating the unknown from time to time.

I hope the many mysteries we have explored in this book has excited your inner seeker — the part of you that stretches the imagination and inspires you to think beyond your current borders of perception.

After all, one of the defining characteristics of being human is our curiosity. It is one of the great natural forces which keeps us moving forward. Use it well.

Bigfoot
&
The Other Ones

Encounters, Stories & Compelling Clues About
Sasquatch & Other Ape-Like Cryptids

By Brian Kingsley

Table of Contents

Introduction

Bigfoot, also called Sasquatch, is thought to be a large, hairy, ape-like being that inhabits some of the dense forests and remote mountain ranges of North America. Although solid, scientific evidence of the creature is lacking, stories of sightings and encounters have been steadily accumulating throughout the years.

As a result, Bigfoot has been placed in the category of so-called "cryptids" — creatures that are thought by some to exist on Earth, but have yet to be properly documented by modern science. Others in this category include the mysterious, waterborne, dinosaur-like being popularly known as "the Loch Ness monster", as well as the goat-eating Chupacabra of South America.

Due to the sheer volume of eyewitness accounts involving Bigfoot, most people in the Western hemisphere recognize the general description of this elusive, ape-like creature. What few may realize, however, is that the Sasquatch is not unique to North America. Or, at least, stories of mysterious, bipedal hominids are not.

From the mountainous regions of Nepal to the wild outback of Australia, tales of such beings have existed throughout history. In many cases, the descriptions of these creatures seem to match Bigfoot.

So, then, a few questions naturally arise:

Are these all part of a singular, long-lost species of great ape, or are they separate beings with different genetic lineages?

How similar are they to each other, where do they to live, and is there any evidence of their existence?

In this book, we will explore these questions, and many more, as we go through fascinating accounts of sightings, encounters and possible findings relating to the many mysterious ape-men of our world.

Chapter 1

The Case For Hidden Hominids

Before we begin our exploration of Bigfoot and the others, let us first tackle one of the most common objections you will hear when discussing the possible existence of these beings.

By now, there has been several hundred years of reported sightings and encounters. Why, then, is there still no solid evidence of Bigfoot or the other, ape-like cryptids that supposedly live on our planet?

Cryptozoologists are generally hopeful that the advent of easily-accessible, high-definition cameras will lead to clear footage of the elusive beings. Many skeptics however, believe that if there has not been produced anything yet, it is likely comprised of nothing but myths and hoaxes.

However, those with such attitudes would do well to remember the many animals that were once thought of as nothing but fantasy. Many species, which are commonly included in text books today, were not even thought to exist just a handful of generations ago. In regards to Bigfoot, the most relevant example of such an animal is the gorilla.

Since Ancient times, European travelers would return home from Africa with stories of huge, hairy, man-like beasts with incredible strength. The very first historical reference to gorillas is thought to come from Greek texts that documented the life of Hanno the Navigator — a famous Carthaginian explorer. He described them as "savage people covered in hair", which his interpreters called "gorillae" — this is where the common name originates from.

In 1559, an English adventurer named Andrew Battel was sailing with one Captain Abraham Cocke towards the Río de la Plata — a partially-closed coastal body where the Uruguay and Parana rivers meet.
Before they could make it all the way there, however, they were forced to return to the Brazilian coastline due extreme wind and hunger.

After desperately docking at São Sebastião, what is today Rio De Janeiro, Andrew Battel and five other men were separated from the rest of the ship's crew. In their vulnerable state, a group of Brazilian Natives captured them and handed them over to the Portuguese who ruled over the region.

After this incident, Battel would spend almost a decade of his life either being imprisoned by, or in service of, the Portuguese. During his time spent traveling with his captors, he would visit several areas of West Africa, where he witnessed gorillas for the first time in his life.

He described them as powerful, human-like monsters that were covered in hair, expect on their faces and ears. He also noted that they had huge fangs, but did not eat any flesh — only fruits, nuts and other plant foods.

Despite Battel's stories of the gorilla, however, the great ape remained largely a mystery for Westerners, and scientists believed the animal to be nothing more than a myth conjured up by African natives.

It was not before 1847 that hard evidence finally surfaced, when the American physician and missionary Thomas Savage sent several gorilla bones, including a skull, from Liberia to a colleague back home. By late summer of that same year, the bones had been carefully examined by several professionals.

Together with Savage's notes on the animals' behavior, the gorilla bones allowed him and the Harvard anatomist Jeffries Wyman to publish a scientific paper officially acknowledging the creature's existence. This would prove to be one of the most important discoveries of the latter part of the century, since the findings played a key role in the soon-to-be heated debate regarding Darwinian evolutionary theory.

Another animal once thought of as mythical is the giant panda of China. Today, it is one of the most iconic creatures on the face of the Earth. In previous centuries, however, they had more or less the status of Bigfoot — few people had seen them, and tales of the animals' existence sounded ridiculous to most.

Giant, docile, black and white bears that ate nothing but vegetation? 'Nonsense', was the general consensus of Western scientists. And, for a long time, it looked to be just that. Besides some rare reports of sightings and the odd story from locals, no hard evidence was found until 1869, when a French missionary named Armand David sent a skin of a dead panda back to Europe.

Still, with expeditions actively searching for pandas in the dense bamboo forests of China, nobody managed to find a live specimen to observe or capture.

It was not until 1916 that a German zoologist named Hugo Weigold managed to locate and purchase a cub from a local while traveling throughout China. He became the first European in history to witness a living panda.

20 years later, in 1936, the American fashion designer and socialite, Ruth Elizabeth Harkness, along with a team of trained professionals, managed to find and capture a nine-week old panda cub in the Chinese wilderness, which they named Su Lin. Su Lin became the first living panda to be sent to a Western country, and spent the rest of her life in the Brookfield Zoo in Chicago.

An interesting detail is that not only were pandas completely unknown outside of China for the past centuries, but even in the natives' own documents and artistic works, there is little mention of the animals. In fact, Chinese artists have been regularly depicting bears and bamboo forests for thousands of years, yet no panda was clearly illustrated until the 20th century.

Other notable mentions of supposedly-mythical creatures that turned out to be real include: giant squids, pythons, Komodo dragons, and even giraffes. With so many animals remaining obscure for centuries, it is certainly not unreasonable to think that one or more intelligent species of ape-like beings are living secluded in the deep forests and underground areas of our planet.

Chapter 2

Bigfoot

Bigfoot, also known as Sasquatch, is generally described as a big, muscular, bipedal, ape-like creature. It is almost fully covered in black, dark brown, or dark-reddish hair, expect on its face, hands and feet. It stands between 6 to 9 feet in height, which places it among the larger of the hominid cryptids that have been reportedly seen around the world.

Those who claim they have seen Bigfoot describe a low-set, large forehead, pronounced brow ridge, and big, dark eyes. The top of his head is crested and round, similar to that of a gorilla.

The large footprints that give the being its popular name have been described as being as long as 24 inches and as wide as 8 inches. Many who have had encounters with him remark on a very strong, musky and unpleasant odor that is impossible to miss.

Bigfoot is usually spotted in forested areas — often in the Pacific Northwest region of the United States and

Canada. Though, he has also been seen in the Great Lakes region of the U.S. Based on the number of sightings reported, it has been estimated by some researchers that between 1500 to 4000 Sasquatch live somewhere in the Pacific Northwest.

Those who have witnessed the beings believe that they are mainly nocturnal, since most sightings and encounters have occurred at night. Based on witness reports, they are also believed to be omnivorous — targeting plants as well as smaller animals for food.

It is not known how Bigfoot communicates, except that they occasionally howl with incredible power — emitting sounds like "ook-ook-ook" and "sooka-sooka" over long distances. In a few cases, they have reportedly slammed rocks and other objects into trees, creating loud thuds at regular intervals, as if they were signaling to each other — or, perhaps, trying to ward off human intruders.

Reports of North American Bigfoot sightings date all the way back to the mid 1800's. However, if we include the earliest Sasquatch tales from Native American folklore, they go back even further. Since these stories are based entirely on oral traditions, though, no one has been able to estimate the earliest mention of the creatures.

According to one of the Native American tribes with the richest Bigfoot lore, the Sts'ailes, the ape-like being's extremely-elusive nature is said to come from some sort of paranormal ability. They believe that the Sasquatch can shift between the physical and spiritual realms, and that, because of this, it is nearly impossible to track down or capture it.

One of the earliest, and most prominent, possible mentions of Bigfoot can be found in a book from 1893 called "The Wilderness Hunter", written by none other than the former U.S. president Theodore Roosevelt.

In his book, Roosevelt relays the story of a fellow outdoorsman he had met on his travels — a German-born man he simply referred to as Bauman. He was a rugged, self-sufficient individual that had lived all his life out on the frontier — areas of the United States that had still not been fully explored or settled by Europeans at the time.

One night, after a hunting trip, Bauman and a friend of his, who remained unnamed, were returning to their camp. As soon as they arrived, it became clear that someone, or something, had ransacked their belongings. Supplies and gear had been thrown around, their lean-to shelter had been torn down, and large footprints could be seen all around the site.

At first, the men suspected that a bear had gone through the area. However, when examining the footprints with a torch, it became apparent that a bipedal creature of some sort had made them — or, at least, that was what it looked like. At that point, it was too dark for the men to be completely sure.

After they had eaten, they spent some time discussing the nature of the tracks and whether or not they could belong to a person. After agreeing on the fact that they looked non-human, the two men rolled up in their blankets and went to sleep. However, their rest would not last long.

Around midnight, Bauman was suddenly awoken by some noise near the camp and quickly sat up with his eyes peeled. Immediately, he noticed a strong smell

— which he described as a "wild-beast odor". Then, he caught a glimpse of a giant, upright figure looming near the opening of the shelter.

Startled, Bauman immediately grabbed his rifle and fired off a shot towards the threatening shadow. The being seemed to have avoided the bullet, and quickly ran off into the woods at incredible speed.

Bauman noted that the creature, whatever is was, could be heard crushing shrubs and small trees as it made its way through the terrain — indicating that it was very heavy. Terrified, the two trappers stayed awake for most the night, only dipping in and out of sleep on occasion. They neither saw nor heard any further sign of the humungous beast, figuring the rifle shot had scared it away.

The next day, they set out into the wilds to check on the traps they had laid the day before, and to set up new ones. When they returned to their camp in the evening, they found that, once again, their equipment had been tossed around and their shelter had been destroyed. Just like the last time, they saw large tracks all around the area — seemingly made by a bipedal creature. The uninvited visitor had been at it again.

Not wanting a repeat of the night before, the men lit a campfire and kept guard one at a time while the other slept. Around midnight, what seemed to be the same creature as earlier appeared on the other side of a stream that ran next to the men's resting place.

It stayed there for a while, partially hidden by shrubs and trees. Since the weather was calm, the men could easily hear branches crack underneath the beast's feet as it moved about. Though it did not come near their campfire, the creature gave off a loud sound every now and again, which Bauman described as a grating, long-drawn groan with a sinister tone.

The following morning, the two men decided to leave the area, as it became obvious that the large creature was displeased with their presence, and that it kept a close eye on them. Before they could move on, however, they needed to check the animal traps they had set out the previous day.

In light of the situation, they agreed to stick together while doing so. After circling the forest to collect most of the traps, which to their dismay were empty, the men were nearing their basecamp once again.

It was now noon, and the sun was shining bright in the sky. Because of this, they figured it was more or less safe to move about. They agreed that Bauman would go alone to check the beaver traps, which were the only ones that remained. In the meantime, his partner would head back to camp to prepare their packs for travel. And, so, they split up.

Hours later, Bauman had finished with the beaver traps, which, to his disappointment, were also empty. He returned to the camp, shouting at his friend from a distance, telling him to get up so they could leave — but he got no answer. As Bauman went closer to the camp, he could see that the fire had gone out.

When he got all the way there, a horrifying scene awaited him. There was his friend, sitting by the trunk of a downed tree, dead. His neck had been viciously broken, and four large fangs looked to have pierced his throat.

When Bauman checked the body of his deceased companion, he noticed that it was still warm. Terrified, he started running as fast as he could, leaving his equipment and gun behind. After fleeing for some time, he finally reached a group of grazing ponies, quickly mounted one of them, and rode it throughout the night until he had left the area completely. And so, the story ends.

It is worth considering that Roosevelt was impressed with the detail and sincerity of Bauman's story, though he noted that, in his opinion, Bauman's German upbringing may have rendered him vulnerable to superstition.

Nevertheless, the former president included it in his book as a legitimate, though unexplained, account of something that actually took place. Whether this ordeal was a legitimate Bigfoot encounter or a misinterpreted run-in with a grizzly bear is still debated within the cryptozoology community.

In the latter part of the 20th century, interest in the creature known as Bigfoot grew a great deal. Eventually, it became part of North American popular culture, and was featured in everything from cartoons to figurines.

This great spike in interest was started by an article from the True magazine in December of 1959, which described the discovery of mysterious, huge, human-like footprints that were found in the wilderness of California.

One of the most widely-believed pieces of evidence of Bigfoot is the "Patterson-Gimlin film" — a 16-millimeter motion picture that seems to show a large, ape-like creature crossing a forest clearing. The being, nicknamed "Patty", seemed to be around 7 feet tall, had a muscular body almost completely covered in hair, wide, low-set shoulders, and very long arms.

Additionally, it had prominent, pendulous breasts, which indicated that it was an adult female. Its proportions, gait and overall look was decidedly non-human, and matched most eyewitness reports of Bigfoot.

The footage was originally shot in Northern California in 1967 by filmmakers Roger Patterson and Robert Gimlin.

Since then, countless groups and individuals have tried to authenticate or debunk it. As new technology became available, the footage was eventually enhanced and stabilized. This revealed certain elements of the film that were previously hard to make out.

One of the things that stuck out the most was the fact that Patty's leg and back muscles can be seen moving underneath her body hair as she walks. This gives the footage a greater sense of authenticity, as it would be extremely hard to fake, especially during the 1960's.

Dmitri Donskoy, formerly Chief of the Dept. of Biomechanics at the USSR Central Institute of Physical Culture, was one of the professionals who examined the Patterson footage.

He concluded that the subject in the film was non-human, based on its peculiar gait and seemingly-heavy body weight — which he said would be nearly impossible to replicate. Donskoy noted that the gait looked natural due to its effortless and confident nature, which he described as "neatly expressive".

The American anthropologist Grover Kantz was

initially very skeptical of the Patterson film, based on the still photos he saw in a magazine. However, after carefully studying the footage himself, he was intrigued by the realism of Patty's locomotion.

He also observed the incredible width and low position of the shoulders, as well as the unique leg and foot motion — which Kantz stated could not have been duplicated by a man wearing a suit. In the end, he concluded that the film showed a real, unknown creature of some sort.

Although certain people, like the costume-seller Philip Morris, said the footage was a hoax which they played some part in making, none of them were able to substantiate their claims. To this day, the Patterson-Gimlin film remains one of the most intriguing pieces of evidence around — not only in the arena of Bigfoot, but paranormal topics in general.

Roger Patterson died of cancer in 1972. Until the end of his days, he insisted that the film was authentic. Robert Gimlin, who mostly shied away from the media, also stood by the fact that the footage was genuine. In 2005, when he finally began appearing at conferences and giving interviews, his story remained unchanged.

Sightings of, and even direct encounters with, creatures thought to be Sasquatch continues to this day. One such encounter reportedly took place in the state of Michigan in November of 2015. In an interview with the Sasquatch Chronicles podcast, a local hunter named Zack told of his unexpected meeting with a giant, ape-like being in the Michigan woods.

It was about 4:30 in the afternoon. Zack was out in the wilds hunting for deer, but had come up empty-handed so far. As it was getting darker, he decided to head towards one of his most trusted hunting spots. He made his way halfway up a very steep hill and hid behind a large stump, aiming his shotgun downwards in preparation for any incoming deer. Unfortunately for him, none showed up.

After some time, he noticed that the area had become strangely quiet. Suddenly, a huge, black, humanoid shape appeared in the corner of his eye. Zack estimated that the creature was about 9 feet tall. It moved in giant strides up the steep hill, seemingly without much effort. The hunter noted that it almost looked like the being was "on a ramp, going up".

The stench was awful, he said — like a mix between rotting meat and a pack of wet dogs. The being's body was covered in thick hair, its arms were very long, and it had an inhuman amount of dense muscle mass. These are all common descriptions of the Sasquatch of North America.

When it reached the top of the hill, the creature was no more than 15 feet away from Zack. Then, it turned its head and made direct eye contact with him. Zack wanted to run, but found himself completely frozen in fear.

What he was looking at became burned into his memory. The Sasquatch's face was partially covered in long, thick hair. Its nose was wide and sunken with large nostrils. The creature's eyes were yellowish green and had a slightly-tired look, which gave Zack the impression that it was sick.

After the brief, but intense, eye contact between the two, the Bigfoot quickly turned around and continued upwards — disappearing into the darkness of the forest. When the encounter had ended, Zack sat by the stump immobilized for several minutes, before finally making a run for his car.

When he reached the safety of the road, he immediately collapsed and vomited profusely — he was left physically and emotionally drained by the entire ordeal. Suffice to say, Zack now believes fully in the existence of Bigfoot, and always stays alert whenever he is out and about in the woods.

Besides the Patterson-Gimlin film and the large number of eyewitness reports, there have been other clues, such as footprint castings, audio recordings of beastly howls, as well as photos and video of what seems to be Bigfoot (though, admittedly, a lot of them are most likely hoaxes or misidentifications). All in all, there is no shortage of circumstantial evidence for the existence of Sasquatch.

With that being said, nobody has managed to record a video of the creature that matches the caliber of the 1967 Patterson-Gimlin film. As a result, the footage remains the most popular piece of Bigfoot evidence even to this day.

Will we ever see something as striking as the Patterson film, but captured with modern, high-definition cameras? Only the future will tell. For the time being, however, the giant, enigmatic ape-man of North America remains well-hidden from humanity.

Chapter 3

Yeti

The Yeti, sometimes referred to as the Abominable Snowman, is a hominid cryptid thought to inhabit the mountainous regions of Nepal and Tibet. According to eyewitness reports, its size and shape are very similar, if not identical, to the North American Bigfoot.

The "mountain man", as he is also called, is said to be ape-like in appearance and considerably taller than the average human. To many, he is an integral part of both Tibetan and Nepalese mythology. In the 19th century, the Yeti quickly became a more well-known creature in Western culture after Bigfoot had entered the mass consciousness with a bang.

Not surprisingly, the giant cryptid is generally regarded by mainstream scientists as nothing but a legend, since there is no conclusive evidence of its existence. Among cryptozoological circles, however, there are serious, ongoing investigations and debates about the mysterious being.

Based on eyewitness reports, it is believed to make its dens in hidden caves, high in the mountains — most of which are inaccessible to humans on foot. Like Bigfoot, the Yeti is also said to be a nocturnal creature, since sightings most often occur at night.

The ape-like beast is largely thought to be an omnivore. Though it relies mostly on meat out of necessity, it has also been seen pulling at branches, bushes and shrubs, seemingly looking for plant foods to eat.

The Yeti was sighted long before the 19th century — even pre-Buddhists believed in its existence. Some worshipped the creature as a God of their hunts, or as a "glacier being". Believers in the Bön religion, an offshoot of Tibetan Buddhism, once thought that the Yeti's blood could be used in some religious ceremonies. As such, it is prominently featured in their traditions.

The first documented, alleged Yeti sighting by a Westerner occurred in 1925, by N.A. Tombazi, a Greek photographer, who was part of a geological expedition from England that was traversing the Himalayan Mountains. Near the Zemu Glacier, he saw a large figure walking across the lower slopes of the mountains in the distance.

It was only about 300 yards away from Tombazi, who described it as a distinctly-humanoid being that was walking upright. He reported that the figure would stop now and then to pull at, or completely uproot, various bushes and other growths. Compared to the snow around it, the creature was dark in color, and wore no discernable clothing.

Tombazi himself did not believe in the Yeti, but was greatly puzzled by the strange figure walking about, apparently naked, in the harsh Himalayan weather. Although the size and behavior of the individual were unusual, Tombazi maintained that it must have been a traveling hermit.

A more direct encounter with a Yeti happened in 1938. One Captain Verner D'Auvergne, who was also a museum curator, was traveling alone in the Himalayas when he suddenly went snow blind during an unrelenting snowstorm. With his vision impaired, he quickly became lost in the freezing terrain.

He stated that, as he was nearing death due to hypothermia, a 9-foot tall being that looked like a pre-historic human, covered head to toe in whiteish-grey hair, rescued him. The creature sheltered him in a cave, fed him and looked over him until he regained his strength. When the captain became healthy enough to make sense of the situation and his surroundings, the supposed Yeti had disappeared.

The most famous incident in the history of Yeti research took place in 1951. British mountaineering legend, Eric Shipton, and the medical doctor and researcher, Michael Ward, were exploring the slopes of the Menlung Glacier, near the border between Nepal and Tibet.

They were both experienced adventurers, and had been part of several demanding expeditions up Mount Everest. This time, they found themselves at an altitude of about 20.000 feet, searching for another route up the famous mountain, when they suddenly spotted a series of strange, deep prints in the snow. The men followed the tracks for about a mile before they finally disappeared on ice.

When they examined the tracks closer, they could see that they looked to be made by large, human-like feet, but with a kind of strange, thumb-like appendage — something between a human and a primate.

They were decidedly enormous — around 13 inches across. To demonstrate this, Shipton placed his trusty ice pick next to one of the footprints as a size comparison and proceeded to take a photograph of it.

As opposed to most Bigfoot tracks which tend to be discovered in muddy terrain, these ones were found in hard snow.

Because of this, the imprints were distinct and highly detailed. This fact, combined with the authority of Shipton and Ward, caused the media to take interest in the men's story and photographs. As a result, the Yeti was quickly thrust into British popular culture.

Since then, there have been several attempts by various explorers and research groups to locate the Yeti. One of the biggest expeditions were funded by the London Daily Mail in 1954, which set out to locate and bring back a Yeti to England.

They were gone for 15 weeks and were accompanied by trained zoologists, ornithologists, and hundreds of attendants who carried tranquillizer guns and a huge cage with them.

Despite their sizable operation, however, they returned home empty-handed. Even so, they did locate some footprints, strange droppings and parts of skin that could not be recognized by experienced analysts.

Sir Edmund Hillary, a mountaineer and explorer

from New Zealand, became the first to climb the great Mount Everest in 1953. He told of several instances where he came into contact with a Yeti. On his record climb up the mountain, both his Sherpa guide and he, himself, observed gigantic, humanoid footprints while ascending the peak.

In 1960, Hillary led a much-anticipated Yeti expedition, traveling with the well-known journalist and author, Desmond Doig. Much like the London Daily Mail expedition in 1954, this quest was also sponsored by a famous name — the World Book Encyclopedia. This gave it a sense of legitimacy that most other expeditions lacked.

The crew brought with them special cameras for infrared and time-lapse photos, as well as expensive trip-wire equipment. Even though they stayed in the area for 10 months, they did not find evidence that would convince anyone that the Yeti exists.

Sir Edmund did bring back a scalp and two skins, which he thought might be from the back of a Yeti's head. Much to his dismay, however, it was revealed after further study that they were actually from two bears and a goat.

After their expedition ended with disappointing results, Doig and Hillary determined that the Yeti must simply be a legend. At a later date, however, Doig stated that he felt their expedition had been far too clumsy.

No Yeti had been spotted — that much was true. But, even with the many people that tagged along, they also did not observe other animals like snow leopards, whose existence is not in dispute.

Westerners are not the only ones that have launched expeditions to locate the Yeti. In 2008, a group of seven Japanese adventurers and researchers went to the Himalayas to look for the cryptid. Their prime goal was a lofty one — to get clear video footage of the elusive beast, in order to prove its existence once and for all.

After a 42-day stay in the freezing mountains, however, they had failed to produce any such evidence. Still, they did not go home completely empty-handed, as they found, and took photographs of, some strange tracks in the snow, which were about eight inches long and looked very human-like.

While skeptics claimed they belonged to different types of bears, the leader of the search party, Yoshiteru Takahashi, insisted that the tracks did not belong to any known animal of the region. The footprints, along with the many accounts from locals he had interviewed, convinced him that the elusive mountain beast is real.

In 2014, a series of studies lead by Bryan Sykes, an Oxford University geneticist, showed that alleged Yeti hairs from the Bhutan and Lahadk regions of the Himalayas contained DNA similar to that of a prehistoric creature reminiscent of a polar bear, which is believed to have existed between 40.000 and 120.000 years ago.

This may show that the Yeti, somehow, is the result of a kind of genetic engineering, or that the mysterious hominid is, in fact, nothing but a long-lost species of bear that occasionally walks on its hind legs.

Alternatively, of course, the hairs that were sent to Sykes and his team may not be from a Yeti at all. The cryptid may still be real, but has mostly avoided leaving behind physical evidence for us to find.

The group who examined the unknown hairs, the Oxford-Lausanne Collateral Hominid Project, also studied alleged samples from other ape-like cryptids, including Bigfoot and the Orang Pendek of Indonesia. The research that has been made public so far, however, has proven to be inconclusive.

Chapter 4

Mapinguary

The Mapinguary, sometimes called Maricoxi, are legendary cryptids located in Brazil that are said to resemble great apes, much like their North American "relatives", Sasquatch. They are said to have red fur, and are different than other creatures described in the native mythology.

Some theories posit that these beasts have clear hominid features, while others state they are more similar to a sloth, due to the long claws that have been observed in some cases.

The Mapinguary is said to have long, powerful arms, which, together with its enormous claws, can tear even palm trees apart.

It has a back that slopes a bit, and it reaches around 7 feet in height. It is completely covered in matted, thick fur, and is sometimes referred to as "blonde beast" in the area of Patagonia.

It is believed that the Mapinguary lives in Bolivia and
Brazil, in the deepest regions of the dense rainforest.
It is allegedly quite slow, but is still considered to be
dangerous since it moves almost silently through
thick vegetation with ease.

Some who have seen the Mapinguary say that it emits
a frightening shriek and gives off a foul stench.
Bullets and arrows seem to be unable to penetrate its
hide, which is similar to that of an alligator. As
opposed to alligators, however, it is believed that the
Mapinguary usually avoids water.

Though most people believe it to be purely mythical,
many cryptozoologists are intrigued by the purported
sightings of this mysterious being. One of the top
theories states that it may be one of the huge, ancient,

sloth-like creatures that are known to have roamed Brazil some time during the Pleistocene era. Many modern sightings seem to hint at this being true.

In 1930, a man named Inocencio was adventuring with his friends in Para State, Brazil, when he became separated from the others. When night fell, he climbed a tree so that he would be safe from the many poisonous and predatory animals that live there.

During the night, Inocencio heard a type of loud cry he had never heard before. Then, he saw a large, black figure that looked somewhat like a man. Terrified, he instinctually took a shot at it, and first believed he wounded it. Suddenly, however, it turned around and rushed away with great speed.

In 1975, a miner named Mario Pereira de Souza said he saw a Mapinguary in the mining camp where he worked. He said it screamed loudly before running on two legs towards his direction.

Curiously, he described the creature as being unsteady on its back feet, and said that it smelled horrible. De Souza was heavily traumatized by the event, and did everything he could to stay away from the rainforest afterwards.

In the 1980's and 90's, an ornithologist and researcher named David Oren managed to locate 50 eyewitnesses who said they had seen a Mapinguary. This group included rubber plantation workers, mine workers and native tribesmen. Seven of those who were interviewed claimed to have gotten shots off at the creature, although no corpse was ever found.

Oren believes that these were giant sloth sightings, and that they prove that the creatures did, in fact, survive the Ice Age after all — though their numbers had likely been heavily reduced. On the other hand, certain Mapinguary sightings describe it in a way that makes it sound similar to the Bigfoot of North America — being hairy, large and bipedal.

Some cryptozoologists believe that both a sloth-like creature and a more traditional, hominid cryptid live somewhere secluded within Brazil. They say that accounts of sightings may have been mixed together under the same name since they share some features, but that they are actually two different types of creatures. Considering how vast and dense the country's wilderness is, this could certainly be possible.

There has been a great deal of effort expended in search of physical evidence of the Mapinguary. Despite of this, there is only the anecdotal kind, at least for now.

During his expeditions, David Oren did find a collection of fur and castings of paws. However, much to his dismay, they were all determined to belong to other, known animals. Even though it has successfully eluded him so far, Oren still believes in the creature's existence.

If we delve into history of the region, we can find evidence that the natives of Brazil may have hunted giant sloths as late as 1895. Footprints, skin and dung that seemed to match the creature were found in an Argentine cave that year.

The Natives reportedly had trouble killing the Giant Sloths because of a bony layer of armor which covered their bodies. The skin found in the cave seemed to match this description. A former governor of Argentina, Ramon Lista, also claimed to have seen a giant sloth in this same area.

The Mapinguary is often mentioned in the folklore of South America's Amazon rainforest. It is sometimes said that the Mapinguary can perform basic speech, which makes some people link it to the South American werewolf mythology.

Certain legends say that the creature was once human, but, for whatever reason, got stuck in a more primitive, animalistic form. Whatever the true nature of the Mapinguary, sightings are still being reported, albeit rarely, to this day.

Chapter 5

Yeren

Some people call the Yeren a "Chinese Bigfoot", but his appearance is actually different from that of the well-known North American cryptid.

The Yeren stands erect, like Bigfoot does, but is reportedly only around 5 to 6.5 feet in height. Its forehead also slopes up from the eyes, as ours do, rather than resembling the typical gorilla-like forehead of the Sasquatch.

Its eyes are said to be deep-set, and the lips protrude. Upturned nostrils and a bulbous nose are also trademarks of the Yeren. Its cheeks are sunken, and its ears are somewhat like a human's, except larger. Its eyes seem to be almost entirely black, and much larger than ours.

The Yeren's body is covered with long, dark brown or reddish hair, except for the areas around the ears and nose. Its legs are relatively close to human proportions, but the arms are markedly elongated — hanging below the knees.

Yeren walk comfortably upright with legs apart, and, based on the footprints that have been found, their feet are roughly 12-19 inches in length.

A smaller hominid, only around 3 feet tall, that looks a lot like the Yeren has reportedly been spotted in China as well. However, some cryptid researchers note that these could simply be children of the same species.

Yeren are said to have raided farms of pigs and chickens in search for food, so they are believed to be omnivorous. Still, there are no reported incidents of them eating human flesh.

Like other hominid cryptids, they choose to run away

and hide rather than attack, and seem to be just as afraid of us as we are of them, if not more so.

Yeren have been in Chinese folklore for centuries, oftentimes they are simply referred to as "Wild Men". Like Bigfoot, they are mainly believed to live in caves in forested, mountainous areas. One of the biggest hotspots of sightings is the Hubei province, which lies in the central part of China.

2000 years ago, a statesman-poet who lived during the Warring States period in China referred to Yeren as "mountain ogres". Later, in the times of the Tang Dynasty, a historian described a band of "very hairy men" roaming around in the region of Hubei. A poet in the Ch'ing Dynasty also described a creature that was much like a monkey, but much larger, and decidedly not a monkey.

Since the Yeren has always been a mysterious and elusive creature, various folk tales naturally began springing up in an attempt to explain it. One of the most popular ones goes like this:

The Chinese emperor who ordered the building of China's Great Wall used compulsory workers to complete the grand project. To escape the forced labor, some of these workers retreated to the deepest areas of the nearby woods.

Legend says that their descendants eventually became hairy, large and wild, but supposedly retained their ability to speak. When we look over the reports of Yeren sightings and encounters, however, there is no mention of any kind of speech — only the occasional guttural sounds and primal screams.

Wang Zelin, a biologist trained at the Chicago Faculty of Biology, is said to have observed the Chinese ape-man in the year of 1940. His group was traveling between cities when the cars suddenly stopped because the drivers heard gunshots ahead. When they arrived at the scene, it was discovered that a Wild Man had been shot and was lying in the road, dead.

Zelin said that the creature was quite tall compared

to the locals — about 6.5 feet. Its body was completely covered with thick, grayish-red hair. When the body of the dead Yeren was rolled over, it was revealed to be a female, with hairy breasts and all. Her appearance was much like the reconstruction of the Chinese Homo erectus — more or less a female "Peking Man".

However, the hair on the dead Yeren was thicker and longer than the recreated model of our old relative. It was also said to have had big, protruding lips. Locals stated that, when alive, it walked briskly and moved about with ease — even up steep hills. It never spoke, but let out a few loud howls now and again. After the incident, Chinese officials arrived at the scene, and nothing was heard about it afterwards.

In 1950, Fan Jingquan, a geologist, had a brief sighting of two Wild Men. He said that they appeared to be a mother and her son. He reportedly saw them in the Shanxi province, in a heavily-forested area that is largely uninhabited by humans.

In 1961, road workers allegedly killed another female Yeren in the Xishuang Banna area. The Chinese Academy of Sciences sent officials to investigate, but the body was gone when they arrived.

They concluded, since the height was claimed to be about 4 feet tall, that it must have been a gibbon instead. 20 years after the fact, however, an anonymous journalist involved in the investigation broke his silence to say that the creature that was killed was, in fact, not a gibbon, but an unknown animal with a human-like appearance.

In 1976, a group of Communist Party members had been driving along a highway in Shennongjia — a mountainous, often misty, area that is covered with dense forest. Out of nowhere, they saw a strange, ape-like creature on two legs, with no tail, covered in reddish hair, in their headlights.

Scared by the men in the car, the creature allegedly tried to grab a nearby branch in order to pull itself off the road. However, in its panic, it failed, and fell to the ground before quickly rushing off into the woods.

To substantiate their story, over 100 members of the Chinese army, including infiltration teams, scientists and photographers descended on the area. They brought with them hunting dogs, tape recorders and guns with tranquilizing darts. Army personnel spent almost two years in the region, speaking with hundreds of locals.

They also formed large search parties in an effort to track down the unknown being. However, as is usually the case with cryptids, even with large groups of people actively hunting, they were unable to locate it. One of the search parties thought they saw a Yeren in one instance, but an accidental shooting reportedly scared the creature away before they could photograph it.

Over 200 footprints were collected between 1980 and 1985 in various locations of the Shennongjia forest. Most of them were around 19 inches long, and the stride was an average of eight feet. Many eyewitness accounts were recorded, but no Yeren was photographed or captured.

Chinese theories lean towards the belief that the Yeren is related to an extinct primate that supposedly lived 300,000 years ago. Some people also suggest that larger specimen of certain monkeys are the real creatures in sightings of the Wild Men.

The animal most often referred to is the golden

monkey — a rare species that could possibly be mistaken for a human-like creature by some observers under confusing circumstances, such as heavy mist.

However, since this animal has a prominent tail, rarely walks upright, and has footprints that are distinctly monkey-like, many cryptid researchers doubt this theory.

Dr. Jeff Meldrum. Professor of the Department of Anthropology at Idaho State University and avid Bigfoot researcher, spoke with eyewitnesses to Yeren encounters and examined two plaster casts of alleged footprints.

He said the prints showed the stride of a creature with a foot physiology that is different from that of humans. So, everything considered, perhaps the Yeren is actually out there, somewhere in the deep, mist-covered forests of China.

Chapter 6

Chuchunaa

The Chuchunaa are sometimes called "Siberian Snowmen". As opposed to most ape-like cryptids, they have been known to walk around with roughly-cut animal skins worn as clothing.

The name "Chuchunaa" means fugitives or outcasts. The fact that they apparently wear clothing of a primitive sort leads some researchers to theorize that they are different from creatures like Bigfoot and the Yeti.

The typical Chuchunaa is between 6 and 7 feet tall — shaped much like a human. It has a protruding brow, broad shoulders, and different colorations of hair that cover most of its body.

These creatures are reportedly found in parts of Russia and Siberia where there are extreme weather conditions. In some parts of Siberia, they are called Mulen, which means "bandit". This is due to the fact that they are known to raid barns and other farm buildings at night. This leads people to regard them as carnivores, since they seem to be on a constant search for animals, most likely for food.

More alarmingly, some locals claim that this creature sometimes eats human flesh, which is not usually reported when it comes to hominid cryptids. According to eyewitnesses, the Chuchunaa have not shown any signs of well-developed communication skills.

Sightings of these beings were originally documented in 1928. The government of the Soviet Union sent more than one expedition to the Yana and Indigirka river regions to document people's accounts of the supposed ape-like beasts.

Certain investigators concluded that these particular hominids may be among the last links between today's humans and our more simian-like ancestors. Parts of Siberia are still barren of human life today, so this could potentially be the last refuge for a species that does not wish to be discovered.

One legend from China says that the Chuchunaa lived in the mountainous Russian region of Verkhoyansk — an area known for its extremely low winter temperatures. As the story goes, the Chuchunaa that lived there would catch and slaughter reindeer, eat them, and then wear their skins on their backs.

Also, the beings were said to have screamed horribly whenever they came across humans — either in fear or as an effort to scare off the intruders.

On the other side of the same mountain range, people reported a discreet creature about 6 feet tall, which observed humans but apparently did not want to interact with them. These beings were mostly seen by fishermen and hunters, who regularly go into areas of the wilderness that other people tend to avoid.

There are also modern-day stories of encounters with the Chuchunaa. In 2002, a Russian newspaper ran a story with the title "In Search of the Snowman", which told of two reporters tracking the Chuchunaa. In the Barylas district, an animal that could not be identified was caught in a wolf trap earlier that year.

Unfortunately, when the trappers arrived, it was already dead. This creature was described as looking like some sort of primate. Its whole body was covered in fur, except for its face and feet.

It also seemed to have a tail, which is unusual for creatures of this type. Some cryptid researchers have noted, however, that this apparent tail might actually have been part of an animal skin, which, as mentioned, Chuchunaa are known to wear on their backs.

The Russian reporter and her photographer wanted to interview the man who had found the body of the strange being. He had, at the time of the incident, been unable to identify it. Later, he said, the corpse suddenly went missing.

According to the local government officials, the man had buried the corpse. Still, some researchers claim that the Russian government quickly swooped in and took the creature's body themselves. Why they would do so remains unclear.

The Russian reporter and her co-worker traveled for two hours by plane and 12 by automobile on dirt roads but, when they arrived, the man who found the creature was no longer living in the village.

Eventually, however, they managed to locate the

father of the man. He stated that his son had found an animal he did not recognize, with a long tail and an unusual, yellowish coat of fur. He made a sketch of the creature after the corpse allegedly disappeared.

The reporter told the father that the officials claimed his son had buried or hidden the animal, but he flat out denied this. Other residents said that the father had been hesitant to speak about his son's extraordinary finding until the rumors were already circulating in the village.

The reporters could not visit the scene of where the creature was discovered since it lies along the Arctic Circle — one of the coldest areas on the entire Earth.

Roads and air travel into this region are only available during mild weather. This is thought to be one of the reasons why the Chuchunaa is so rarely observed compared to other hominid cryptids.

Most sightings of Chuchunaa come from hunters, reindeer breeders and the older residents that live in the remote areas of Russia. According to these individuals, the creature can catch wild reindeer by creeping on all fours up to a herd, before it leaps and runs swiftly to take one animal down.

As the stories go, when the Chuchunaa catches a reindeer, by grabbing its head or horns, he quickly breaks its neck by shaking it violently. He also sometimes hunts young elk, but does not interact with the largest of the animals.

It appears that, in this particular area, Chuchunaa have hunting grounds in different seasons. They visit the areas of most bitter cold only when the temperatures are moderate. They move to the tundra to follow and hunt the wild deer around springtime, but eventually return to the forest (their preferred location) when the deer herd migrates there in autumn.

To date, there has been no clear-cut physical evidence of the Chuchunaa brought forward for examination. There are plenty of sightings and accounts, but there is no solid proof that backs up their existence. A few photographs have surfaced that have been introduced as evidence, but they cannot be dated or substantiated by any conventional means.

With that being said, in 2005, an archeological group explored the Denisova Cave in Siberia's part of the Altai Mountains. They discovered a fifth phalanx bone in the cave that could point to a new human relative. Curiously, it is different from both Neanderthals and modern humans.

Researchers have dubbed this potential hominid, "X-Woman". One team member described the discovery as ground breaking, since they could have found part of a creature that has not even been on the radar of human development until now.

Ian Tattersall, from New York's American Museum of

Natural History, explains that the family tree of humans has many branches, and that it is entirely feasible that there are branches out here that we do not know about yet. If the Chuchunaa is one of them remains to be seen.

Chapter 7

Barmanu

The Barmanu of Pakistan and Afghanistan is another cryptid believed to be related to early humans. It is often described as a cross between an ape and a man, and its name is simply translated to "hairy one".

Like the Chuchunaa of Russia, it has been spotted wearing animal skins as rudimentary clothing. This rare, but shared, characteristic, combined with their close proximity to each other, leads some researchers to think that Barmanu and Chuchunaa are actually the same species.

The male Barmanu stands a bit over 6 feet in height and are hairier than their female counterparts, who are shorter in stature and have pendulous breasts, much like "Patty" in the Patterson-Gimlin Bigfoot film.

Although their walk is very similar to humans, their bodies are reportedly more muscular. Their arms look long for their height, and their feet are inhumanly big.

The ape-like beings seem to dwell in the Karakoram and Hindu Kush mountain ranges, between the Himalayan and Pamir mountains. Sometimes, they have also been spotted in the Shishi Kuh Valley. Based on eyewitness accounts, Barmanu speech only consists of guttural grunting, but it will occasionally emit higher-pitched shrieks when it is hurt or upset.

It mostly feeds on leaves, roots, fungi, berries and nuts. It is also believed to eat meat on occasion, although it is not known for stealing livestock like the Chuchunaa.

Tales of the Barmanu go back centuries. In the early 1900's, those in Spanish expeditions into Northern Pakistan first learned about the creature from the locals. These stories came to the attention of a Spanish zoologist named Jordi Magraner.

According to those who met him, Magraner had a very serious and scientific way of enquiry. With over a decade of intense research and documentation, he became the first to bring the Barmanu to international attention.

Initially, Magraner traveled frequently in the areas where Barmanu had been sighted, together with a physician, Anne Mallasse, and a third member of the team that remained anonymous. From 1992 through 1994, the three of them chronicled numerous eyewitness reports and personal experiences regarding the Barmanu. They also discovered footprints that appeared like they were made by apes, only larger.

Rahim Shah, an elderly man who lived in the Alai Valley of Kyrgyzstan, explained to Magraner that he had only seen the Barmanu whenever they came down from the mountains to the valley — which only happened during heavy snowfall. He said he had seen them throughout his whole life, and had even witnessed a mother and child holding hands.

His last encounter, he said, occurred in the early morning, just after dawn. He said he was not afraid, since he had seen the same type creature before, and they never acted aggressive towards him. They did not bother him, and he did not bother them. He fondly referred to them as "the big hairy ones", which is what they are often called in Eastern Afghanistan and Northern Pakistan.

In 2002, Jordi Magraner planned to go back to Europe to share his findings about the Barmanu. Before he could do so, however, he was found viciously murdered under mysterious circumstances. According to the local police, Magraner was found lifeless in a small house he was renting in a village near Kailash valley.

It appeared as if his throat had been brutally slit open with a knife. No one was ever convicted of the murder, and the motives remain unclear — though, naturally, different theories exist.

Compared to sightings of Bigfoot, encounters with the Barmanu seem to be more commonplace. Shepherds in the mountains have reported seeing the creatures year after year. They describe encounters as more or less routine occurrences that they expect. However, none of the shepherds, or any investigating zoologist for that matter, has ever discovered a cave or other dwellings in which the creatures might live.

The previously-mentioned mountain man of Alai valley, Rahim Shah, is said to be the person who has seen the Barmanu most frequently. However, not even he has found a single one of their caves or dens. He believes there are fewer Barmanu in existence now, since they are seen less often than they were in his younger years.

A 2005 earthquake may be partially responsible for the lowered number of encounters, since it utterly devastated the area where Barmanu were most often sighted. If they are like most wild animals, the ape-folk may have moved to a safer place as soon as they got a sense of the quake.

Today, there is also more of a government presence in this area than there used to be, which may account for fewer Barmanu sightings. Additionally, many people in Non-Governmental organizations (NGOs) regularly explore the mountains today, making the area less appealing for those who wish to stay hidden.

The nomads who bring herds into the valley for summer month grazing have also had fewer encounters with the Barmanu than they used to have. Some are a bit sad, since they feel that "the big hairy ones" have always been a part of the mountain life. Most local shepherds believe that the Barmanu has the same right to live in the area as they do.

Accounts from eyewitnesses in the area are obviously not enough evidence to sway most skeptics. However, due to the sheer number of sightings in such a small area, it seems highly likely that something out of the ordinary roams this mountainous landscape in the East.

Chapter 8

Almas

Almas, or Almasty, is a singular word in Mongolian which simply means "Wild Man" — referring to the mysterious hominid creature that has been spotted in certain areas of the country. This type of being is said to inhabit the Pamir and Caucasus Mountains in Central Asia, as well as the Altai Mountains in southern Mongolia. On rare occasions, they have also been reported in certain parts of Russia.

Like the Cuchunaa and Barmanu, Almas are usually considered closer to being wild, hairy humans than apes, in both their habits and appearance. This contrasts them with cryptid hominids like the Himalayan Yeti, which is believed to be more beast than man.

Almas are generally described as bipedal creatures standing 5 to 6.5 feet in height. Their bodies are covered with fine, brown-reddish hair. Their facial features include a weak chin, prominent brow-ridge and a flat nose. Almas are generally unclothed, although some people have seen them wearing primitive animal skins as clothing, just like the Chuchunaa and Barmanu.

It is worth noting that the common eyewitness description of the Almas is very similar to the reconstructed models of the Neanderthals. The only big difference seems to be the abundant, thick body hair of the Mongolian Wild Men.

Like most hominoid creatures, the Almas seem to prefer living in forested, hilly or mountainous areas. Unlike most creatures of his type, however, humans living in the surrounding villages describe themselves actually communicating with them, albeit in a primitive way — mostly using hand gestures.

Locals say that the Almas feed mainly on berries and other plant foods, but individual specimen have sometimes been seen hunting animals as well. They are nocturnal, and thus very difficult to spot most of the time. As far as locals know, Almas do not leave any trace of their death in areas frequented by humans.

There is some evidence that suggests that these hominids may be more real than imaginary. This includes many hundreds of eyewitness accounts and findings of strange, human-like footprints. Documented reports of sightings and interactions with Almas go back hundreds of years, and, interestingly enough, the descriptions of the creatures have not changed during that time.

As far back as 1430, Johann Schiltberger, a Bavarian traveler and writer of noble descent, stated that he observed the Almas in Mongolia when he was a captive of a Mongol Khan. When he returned home later in his life, he wrote a book titled "The Bondage And Travels of Johann Schiltberger", relaying his incredible experiences.

In his memoir, Schiltberger clearly mentions the Almas, which he refers to as savages. He said they would "run about like other wild beasts in the mountain", and that they would eat leaves, grass, and whatever they could find. He mentioned that their bodies were covered with hair, except for their hands and faces.

Nikolai Przhevalsky, a Russian geographer and explorer, conducted five major expeditions in his life time; one to the Russian far east, and four to Mongolia, Zinjang and Tibet. During his travels, he documented a number of animals that were unknown to most people outside of these areas.

One such animal was a kind of wild horse, which was the last surviving species that was not widely domesticated by humans. Today, the species is called Przhevalsky horse, named after the Russian explorer.

The horses were not the only new creatures Przhevalsky came upon during his expeditions, however. In 1871, he reported seeing the elusive Wild Men of the mountains himself.

Though he never managed to get close enough to study the strange beings, the Russian explorer was quite serious about their existence. He also noted that these beings were listed in the Tibetan and Mongolian apothecary books, alongside many other plants and animals that are known to exist today.

From 1890 to 1928, a Russian professor named
Tysben Zhamtsarano was purportedly conducting
research into the Almas. As was often the case in
Russia at that time, the scientist was eventually
thrown into a gulag.

His illustrations, notes and other evidence, which is
believed to have been quite extensive, disappeared
along with him. Zhamtsarano's assistant, who
avoided the gulag, claimed that he saw much of the
evidence himself, including the skin of an Almas that
had been preserved in a Buddhist monastery in
Mongolia.

In 1963, another Russian, a children's doctor named
Ivan Ivlov, reported that he saw an entire family of

Almas at a distance of about half a mile. His experience was validated by his personal driver, who also claimed to have observed the Wild Men.

Furthermore, being a pediatrician, Ivan Ivlov regularly spoke to Mongolian children, and many of them said they had also seen the strange hominids. Some even claimed to have interacted with them, and stated that the human and Almas children were not afraid of each other.

Local Mongolian legend tells about a "wild woman" named Zana who once lived in a remote mountain village. Some researchers believe that she might have been an Almas, but there was no hard evidence to confirm this.

As legend tells it, she was captured by humans in 1850. She was at first quite violent, likely in response to her sudden kidnapping, but eventually calmed down and settled into her new surroundings.

After she got accustomed to the village life, she is said to have had a sexual relationship with a local man who she later married. Together with him, she gave birth to several children who appeared to be more or less human.

One of these children were reported to have died during their infancy, allegedly because Zana's genetics were not fully compatible with those of her human partner. According to locals, Zana died in 1890 — though the cause of her death remained unclear.

The story goes on to describe how her husband gave away four surviving children to different families of the village. They were all assimilated into the society and eventually married, each having a family of his or her own.

A physician later examined the skull of one of Zana's children after his death and reportedly found it to be a human skull. If this is true, it is possible that Zana was simply from a tribe of hunter-gatherers, rather than a true Almas. Though, if the children were in fact hybrids, the skulls may have looked more or less human anyway.

A French cryptozoologist, Bernard Heuvelmans, and a British anthropologist, Myra Shackley, speculate that Almas are related to the Neanderthals. Another cryptozoologist, Loren Coleman, has suggested that they may be the only surviving descendants of our upright human relatives — homo erectus.

There are some cryptid researchers who insist that the Almas is closely related to the Himalayan Yeti. The locals, however, see themselves as being not much different to the Almas. They see them as simple Wild Men — untouched by the refining qualities of civilization.

There does exist alleged Almas footprint castings and even some debatable photographs that are circling the internet.

However, no indisputable physical evidence that the Almas exists has ever reached the mainstream scientific community. It is speculated that, like other cryptids, researchers will need to find a whole body, or even capture a live Almas, in order to acknowledge their existence.

In 2003, the ongoing controversy over whether the Almas is real or not was briefly rekindled. The BBC (British Broadcasting Corporation) reported at that time that Sergey Semenov, a mountain climber, had discovered the leg and foot of a creature he could not identify in the high-altitude permafrost region of the Altai Mountains.

X-rays and tests showed that the bones were thousands of years old, but all attempts to identify exactly what creature they belonged to were inconclusive.

Chapter 9

Batutut

The Batutut, or Ujit, of Vietnam is speculated to be either a lost tribe of primitive humans or an undiscovered hominid species like Bigfoot. Based on most eyewitness accounts, it appears to be the latter.

The height of the creatures can vary, from around 5 to over 7 feet tall. Their bodies are almost completely covered in black, brown or gray hair, except on their faces, feet and hands.

According to observers, they walk comfortably upright, much like humans. Vietnamese scholars refer to the creature as Ngoui Rung — which loosely translates to "forest man".

The Batutut seem to forage for most of their food, which usually includes leaves and fruit. From time to time, they also kill and eat small animals, like langurs and foxes, though they prefer to eat snails and mussels for meat.

In general, these creatures don not seem to bear ill will toward humans. In remote villages in Vietnam, they have even been reported to wander up close to campfires and calmly sit nearby.

According to eyewitness accounts, they do not speak, but, like most hominid cryptids, they do occasionally make some strange noises. They seem to know what each one is saying when seen in small groups. According to observers, they have a very dense musculature, which give the tallest of them an imposing presence.

Dang Nghiem Van, an anthropologist in Hanoi, collects Batutut information from Vietnam's central highlands to the northern parts of the country.

Based on what he has uncovered, they are commonly described as extremely powerful yet elusive creatures, and their movement has both human and ape-like characteristics.

The locals believe that Batutut steal people's personal belongings from time to time. They have reportedly even stolen guns, although they have not shown any ability to fire them.

As in most countries, areas of uninhabited wilderness are steadily decreasing in Vietnam, which means, for better or worse, that it should be harder for the creatures to remain in hiding.

In the 1960's, American soldiers deployed in Laotian and Vietnamese jungles encountered strange, scary creatures which they had never seen or heard of before.

One sergeant named Thomas Jenkins was interviewed after reconnaissance missions in Vietnam. He said that in 1969, he saw a group of what looked like big apes throwing rocks at members of his platoon. This incident gave the Batutut their new, Western, name, "Rock Apes".

Jenkins does not believe that the creatures they saw were normal apes or monkeys, even though biologists say there are many of those in Vietnam. Instead, Jenkins insists that these beings were darker in color, walked upright, and were more muscular than simple monkeys.

The creatures the soldiers observed would sometimes wake them up in the morning, screaming, yelling and shaking their fists. Jenkins said it looked a lot like a human behavior, and that it was obvious to everyone that they objected to the presence of soldiers in the jungle. Unfortunately, since most soldiers in the 1960's did not have cameras with them, no one managed to take a photograph of these unknown hominids.

In addition to American soldiers, North Vietnamese fighters also reported what they called "forest people". They stated that the large creatures attacked their soldiers, too. So, it would seem that the so-called Rock Apes did not take any side in the human conflict, but rather wanted all of them gone from their territory.

The Bigfoot researcher Cliff Barackman states that his father told him an interesting story of another American soldier who served in Vietnam. One day, the platoon of this soldier was firing on the North Vietnamese in the deep jungle. Suddenly, a mysterious, humanoid creature walked through a small clearing, before climbing a very steep embankment and disappearing back into the jungle.

The animal apparently scaled the sharp incline easily, which impressed the American soldier. This account echoes many sightings of Bigfoot, which is also known to effortlessly traverse rough wilderness with inhuman speed.

A retired US forces helicopter pilot, Larry Wilson,

allegedly had his own encounter with the Batutut in 1970. He was flying into a valley in the Vietnamese wilderness when he spotted a tree, stripped of its leaves, wiggling fiercely.

He then saw a strange ape-man shaking the tree with astonishing power. Wilson described the creature as having a flat skull, roughly the size of a soccer ball, and facial features similar to humans. He had a clear, unobstructed view of it, and was certain it was part ape and part man.

Searching for Batutut in Vietnam's dense jungles is close to impossible these days. There are plenty of unexploded land mines and bombs from the war that make it extremely dangerous for any person traveling on foot.

The roads also tend to wash out in the rainy season, which make them nearly impassable. Furthermore, the Vietnam jungle is so incredibly dense that you can hardly see a foot ahead, even when several people are clearing with machetes.

Logistics aside, Josh Gates of Destination Truth (an American paranormal reality TV series) went there in an effort to find the Batutut in 2012. He interviewed Dr. Tran Hong Viet, who works at the Cryptozoic Research Center of Vietnam. This institution was initially set up by the government in order to find and study the elusive forest people.

Dr. Viet has researched the case of the unknown ape-beast for over 30 years and is a strong believer in its existence. He found a footprint some years ago in a very remote cave. The print was not that of any known primate, nor was it human. While in Vietnam, Josh Gates took many photographs of the fascinating print, which was shown on the Destination Truth show.

After talking to Dr. Viet and learning about his findings, Gates pondered where to go in order to search for the Batutut. The vast and uninviting Kebang National Park is barely explored, so he decided to take his crew there. While traversing the terrain, they were filming as they went, documenting nearly every step of their journey.

During their time there, something threw a stone at them out of nowhere. Heavy footsteps were also heard rushing towards their direction before suddenly backing off, at the same time as they heard loud, animalistic calls like they had never heard before. Despite these threatening happenings, however, no Rock Ape made a face-to-face appearance with the crew while they journeyed through the jungle.

The highlight of the whole search was a fresh footprint found by Gates, who carefully cast it and brought it home to the U.S. for additional study.

Professor Jeff Meldrum examined Gates' cast and confirmed that it is an authentic sample of an unknown Vietnamese hominoid. These fresh findings give hope to the idea that the mysterious Batutut will eventually be discovered.

Chapter 10

Yowie

In Australia, hairy, hominoid creatures are sometimes interchangeably referred to as either a Yowie or a Yahoo. However, based on eyewitness accounts, these are actually two separate beings with their own unique characteristics.

A Yahoo is described as spending more time on four legs than two. Standing upright, it is about 5 feet in height. It is furry on its sides and back, with lighter-colored fur on its belly, head, arms and legs. Based on sightings, it resembles a thought-to-be extinct type of marsupial that resembled an ape.

The Yowie, on the other hand, is much bigger and stranger looking, and seems to walk comfortably on two legs, like the Yeti and Bigfoot. It appears more human than the Yahoo, but more monster-like as well — due to its huge stature and incredibly-dense musculature. From here on out, we will be speaking mainly about the Yowie.

Yowies are much like other hominid cryptids in that they seem most at home in a forested, mountainous area. In Australia, some of their habitats are flat, while others are hilly. As is the case with similar creatures, people who flee from an encounter with a Yowie have found that when they reach a clearing or road, the creature will stop following them.

On some occasions, Yowies have been seen hunting and killing small pigs and chickens. Most of the time, however, they seem to exist on berries that they pull from branches and on the bark of certain trees, in addition to other plant foods they can find.

Aboriginal folklore has tales of the Yowie that go back for ages, possibly many hundreds of years, if not more. According to the Sydney Morning Herald, the first Western sightings of Yowies occurred in 1795. Back then, they were simply referred to as "indigenous apes".

In 1876, the Australian Town and Country Journal cited Aboriginal beliefs of hairy men who lived in the woods, and who were not animals, yet not quite human.

In 1882, another article mentioned the eyewitness account of a naturalist named Henry James McCooey, who claimed to have seen one of these mysterious apes near the southern coast of New South Wales.

As is the case with most cryptids, reports of Yowie sightings were quite rare, but continued to pile up as the years went by — slowly but surely painting a clear picture of the creature's physical features and habits. In 1982, exactly 100 years after the story of James McCooey was published, another Australian man had an astonishing encounter with a strange, half-human, half-ape being.

The man was walking along the coast of New South Wales when he suddenly heard cries of small birds. When he went to look at what was causing the commotion, he saw that they were darting around a strange-looking creature. The mysterious beast looked to be on its hind legs, but not fully upright, and was looking at the birds that were circling around it. It was blinking its eyes and making a low, chattering noise.

The man was at an elevation higher than the Yowie, so he was easily able to observe its general appearance. He reported that the being would be less than 5 feet in height if it stood upright. It was covered with long hair, which was black, except for reddish patches near the breast and throat. Its eyes were small and partially hidden by some of its matted hair.

The Yowie's arms were slightly longer then its legs — somewhere between a chimpanzee and a human, which is a common indicator of Bigfoot-like beings. The man was initially shocked and repulsed by the creature. Terrified, he threw a rock at the unsuspecting Yowie, which subsequently rushed off — disappearing into a ravine.

As mentioned, this sighting took place in the Australian state of New South Wales. This place has turned out to be somewhat of a hotspot for Yowie encounters, especially near the more mountainous regions, such as the Brindabella Range, which is a popular area for hikers.

In contrast to the North American Sasquatch, the Yowie seems to be more daring when it comes to venturing near humans. While Bigfoot rarely comes anywhere near our territories, Yowies, based on eyewitness accounts, will gladly roam alongside hiking trails or empty cabins. However, that is typically where they stop — they seem to shy away from bright-lit streets, camping grounds and other busy areas.

In 1995, an Australian man named Dean Harrison, formerly a Yowie skeptic, found himself suddenly turned into a believer. He initially figured the stories about the ape-man to be nothing but camp fire tales and jokes for the pub.

He stated that his skepticism abruptly ended after a series of terrifying encounters, which forced him to accept what mainstream science has not: that Yowies are very much real.

Harrison arrived at his home in Queensland late one night in 1995, with no idea that his life was about to be turned upside down. When he got out of his car, he heard a loud commotion near his back fence.

It was a deep growling followed by branches being violently snapped. Harrison went to check it out, before suddenly stopping dead in his tracks. In front of him was a huge, hairy, bipedal beast, crashing around and pulling out small trees from their roots.

Harrison still recalls the hulking creature having a mix of human and ape-like features that he had never seen before. Terrified, he ran into his house and tried to come to terms with what he had just witnessed. Moments later, the Yowie had disappeared.

After the shocking event, Harrison immediately started searching everywhere he could for information about the monster he saw near his backyard.

Much to his dismay, he did not find much information available. In fact, almost every mention of the ape-like being was accompanied by a mocking tone — no mainstream organization took it seriously.

Not wanting to appear as a crazy person or a liar, Dean Harrison kept the encounter to himself and tried to move on. However, two years later, in 1997, Harrison would have his second meeting with a Yowie. This time, things would become much more personal.

It was late at night, and Harrison was jogging in a thicket next to the suburban streets of his hometown of Ormeau, Queensland. Before heading further in, he stopped to talk to his wife on the phone. In the middle of the conversation, he suddenly heard strange noises coming from behind him. Foliage was being parted, and something big was steadily heading his way.

Dean Harrison told his wife that he thought it may be a man trying to sneak up behind him. He ended the call, turned towards the sounds and took a defensive position — readying himself for whatever came through the bushes.

To his surprise, out came a massive, humanoid silhouette — the Yowie had arrived. It quickly spotted Harrison standing there, and slowly and ominously crouched down between the foliage.

Harrison, consumed by the instinct to flee, made a sudden move with his foot. This provoked the Yowie, which then gave off a bestial roar before lunging forward. Immediately, Harrison got a powerful adrenaline rush, and he started sprinting away as fast as he could.

As he ran along a cleared path, the huge beast ran more or less parallel with him. It effortlessly maneuvered its way through the thick forest — evading logs and rocks like they were nothing. Harrison quickly realized that the Yowie was trying to cut him off.

Fearing his life was about to end, he abruptly changed direction, and managed to buy himself just enough time to reach a well-lit road nearby. Realizing the creature was no longer chasing him, Harrison looked back. The massive beast had retreated into some bushes at the edge of the road, once again squatting down partially hidden while staring right at him.

Dean Harrison recounted his impression of the terrifying creature:

"It was so powerful... If this thing had got a hold of me, I wouldn't have time to scream — it would've snapped my neck like a toothpick..."

This second encounter with Australia's mysterious, hulking, ape-man turned Harrison's life upside down. Due to the raw emotional impact, he decided he would now openly discuss and search for the creature. Later that year he founded the Australian Yowie Research Group, and started the website Yowiehunters.com.au.

Since then, he has made it his passion to collect evidence for, and document sightings of, the Yowie. As he speaks to those who claim to have seen the creature, Harrison asks them to sketch what they saw.

He has found that most of the portraits, many of which can be found on his website, are decidedly similar: larger and more muscular than humans, covered in fur that ranges from dark chocolate to reddish brown, with a face that seems to be part man, part ape. This is another reason Harrison believes he saw the same creature they did — the vast majority of the eyewitness descriptions match each other.

Though reports of sightings and close encounters continue to accumulate, hard evidence of the Yowie's existence is still lacking. There are some interesting videos that were allegedly taken of the hulking ape-man, but due to their quality, nothing can be said for certain.

Additionally, there are casts from Australian creek beds that were sent to the United States for examination. Forensic experts confirmed that they are quite similar to the prints of North America's own Bigfoot, which researchers have been casting for years. As is the case with other hominid cryptids, however, these imprints alone will not sway most skeptics.

Dean Harrison notes that since technology is changing at a rapid pace, the chances of getting footage of the Yowie will increase. He hopes that, with the advent of high-definition dash cams and smart phones, clear footage of the massive beast will eventually emerge.

Chapter 11

Orang Pendek

"Orang Pendek" means "short person" in Indonesian. This is the name given to a small, hominid cryptid that is believed to live in the jungles of Sumatra — a large island located in western Indonesia.

It is described as an ape-like being that stands 3 to 6 feet tall, with a powerful, humanoid physique that separates it from the rest of the local animal life. It is almost completely covered in short, brown, golden or greyish hairs, and moves around efficiently on two legs.

Its name is indeed reminiscent of the well-known orangutan, which translates to "person of the forest". However, according to eyewitness testimony, the Orang Pendek has facial features that are more similar to those of humans rather than apes or monkeys.

Orang Pendek are reported to be non-aggressive in most cases — it prefers to hide away in the deepest corners of the Sumatran jungle. However, when they have come in contact with humans, they have been known to stretch their arms into the air while making guttural sounds —a common tactic primates use when trying to appear more threatening.

The diet of the Orang Pendek is said to consist mainly of plant foods like young shoots, durian fruit, and ginger roots. Given the opportunity, it will also feed on insects or smaller animals, like crabs.

Occasionally, the stocky ape-men have been observed helping themselves to a farmer's harvest. They seem to particularly enjoy corn, as well as all kinds of fruit.

The Orang Rimba (meaning "people of the forest"), also called Suku Anak Dalam (translated to "Children of the Inner-forest"), is a group of indigenous, animist peoples that live throughout the dense Sumatran forests. According to them, the upright ape-men have been living in the wilderness for centuries.

The Orang Rimba elders know where most of the Orang Pendek territories lie, and will occasionally leave behind offerings for them. They do not see the creatures as mysterious or threatening at all. To them, they are simply one of the many co-inhabitants of the forest.

While the tribes of the forest are not typically afraid of the Orang Pendek, the everyday people of the surrounding villages have a different relationship with the hairy beings. They view them as intelligent creatures with a near-supernatural ability to hide from humans. This makes many villagers afraid of the Orang Pendek — they make sure to watch their backs whenever they are walking in what they perceive to be "short people" territory.

From a Western perspective, the Orang Pendek was first heard about in the beginning of the 1900's, when Indonesia was still a Dutch colony referred to as the Dutch East Indies. In 1917, the Dutch Sumatran governor received reports of an unknown hominoid creature living in the dense forests of the island. One of the most peculiar documented cases was that of a Dutch plantation owner simply referred to as Mr. Oostingh.

While he was walking through the forests near the Bukit Kaba mountain in Sumatra, Oostingh suddenly spotted a strange creature sitting on the ground, approximately 30 feet away from him. The being, he said, was about as large as a medium-sized native Indonesian, but with extremely thick, square, shoulders. Also, its body was completely covered in hair, with a dusty, almost grey, blackish color.

Oostingh recalled his experience with the Orang Pendek as follows:

"He obviously noticed my presence. He did not turn his head, but stood up on his feet: he seemed about as tall as I am, about 1.75 meters. Then I realized that this was not a man, and I started back away since I was not armed.

The creature took several paces and then, with his long arm, grasped a small tree, which seemed to almost break under his weight, before quietly springing into a larger tree, swinging in great leaps to the right and to the left.

My main impression was, and still is, 'what a huge beast!' It was not an orangutan — I had seen one of those apes before at the Artis, the Amsterdam Zoo. It was more like a monstrously-large siamang, but a siamang has long hair, and there was no doubt this one had short hair. I did not see its face since, indeed, it never looked at me once."

6 years later, in 1923, while surveying land in Sumatra, another Dutch settler named Van Heerwaden sighted a similar creature of unknown origin. He reportedly saw what looked to be some kind of ape sitting on the branch of a nearby tree. It was unlike anything he had ever seen before.

He described it as dark and extremely hairy, but with facial features that were neither ugly nor ape-like in appearance. Van Heerwaden noted, however, just like Oostingh, that the being had very long arms, which would reach just a little above its knees if it stood up. Also, its legs seemed to be very short.

These two factors combined made its body look decidedly non-human. Furthermore, while the settler could not make out the creature's feet, he could see its toes, which he said were quite normal-looking — meaning, they looked much like ours.

Van Heerwaden's detailed observations are typical of most Orang Pendek sightings. Talk about elongated arms can certainly make casual skeptics conclude that they are nothing but orangutans viewed at an obfuscating angle.

However, two peculiar things that seem to stick out the most are the feet and faces of these beings. They give onlookers the distinct feeling that they are not witnessing a common ape or monkey. Instead, it regularly conjures up feelings of amazement or fear that no everyday animal can.

When it comes to modern Orang Pendek research, Debbie Martyr, a former English journalist, is the most notable. She spent over two decades doing wildlife conservation work and research in Sumatra, promoted and funded by Fauna and Flora

International — a global non-governmental organization.

During her stay in the region, Martyr interviewed hundreds of witnesses who claimed to have seen the Orang Pendek. One of her team members, a professional wildlife photographer named Jeremy Holden, also set up various camera traps in the areas where the ape-man had reportedly been spotted.

Debbie Martyr and her team documented many rare animals in Sumatra, and even rediscovered a lost species of deer — the muntjac, which had not been seen since 1930.

Despite their many successful ventures, however, the team never managed to get a clear photograph of the Orang Pendek. Even so, several of them claim to have personally witnessed the rare hominoid at several occasions.

Debbie Martyr reportedly got her first glimpse of the creature in 1990 — only one year after arriving in Sumatra for the first time. She described the being as a relatively small, though immensely powerful-looking, non-human primate. She noted that it did not look like an orangutan, since its proportions did not match.

The creature was built much like a boxer, she said,

with immense upper-body strength. It had a beautiful color, and moved bipedally in an efficient manner while trying to avoid being seen by the humans.

Jeremy Holden did not have such a direct sighting, but caught a glance of the Orang Pendek while it went over a hill, deep inside the Sumatran forest. He saw the being from behind as it swiftly made its way through the wilderness. Like Martyr, Holden noted that the creature moved upright — more like a human than an ape.

In September of 2001, a team of three independent British explorers and cryptozoologists — Adam Davies, Andrew Sanderson and Keith Townley — traveled to Sumatra to search for evidence of the Orang Pendek.

In the three weeks they were there, they did not see the creature themselves. However, they did find some compelling evidence near Kerinci — a Sumatran volcano surrounded by dense, lush forests.

While they were scouring the area, Davies and his team spotted a set of strange footprints in the muddy ground, which they proceeded to make a cast out of. Nearby, they also found some peculiar, long strands of hair that were yellow-brown in color.

Excited, the crew traveled home with their findings. They gave the footprint cast to Cambridge Professor Dr. David Chivers, who compared it to other known Sumatran animals. He deduced that it was definitely from some sort of ape, which seemed to have a mix of characteristics from humans and other known hominids.

Dr. Chivers' final statement on the matter was as follows:

"From further examination, the print did not match any known primate species, and I can conclude that this points towards there being a large, unknown primate in the forests of Sumatra".

The strange hairs that the three men found were sent to an expert on mammal hairs, Dr. Hans Brunner, at Deakin University in Melbourne, Australia. After performing extensive DNA testing, he determined that the hairs found in the Sumatran jungle did not match any of the known local animals, nor did they belong to a human. His final statement was that the hairs seemed to belong to an unidentified type of primate.

At the start of 2005, National Geographic provided funding for a project aimed at getting photographic evidence of the Orang Pendek. It was led by Dr. Peter Tse from Dartmouth College, New Hampshire, and involved placing a number of camera traps in the regions where the cryptids had been commonly sighted. Unfortunately, the project concluded in 2009, after many years of frustration due to lack of success.

Today, despite the intriguing footprints and hair samples found in 2001, there are still no clear photographs or video footage of the mysterious Orang Pendek. However, as eyewitness accounts continue to pile up, many researchers still believe its existence can be proven in the future.

Conclusion

Now you know about some of the most astonishing sightings, encounters and evidence of the world's many mysterious ape-like creatures. By examining the eyewitness descriptions, it is clear that some of them, like the Yeti, Yowie, and Bigfoot, seem very similar, if not identical, while others, like the Almas and Orang Pendek, seem to stand out from the crowd.

However, if we assume that the beings are, in fact, real, all of them certainly share an exceptional ability to stay hidden from humans. Untold numbers of expeditions, both by independent actors and big organizations, have been launched in an effort to find Bigfoot and the others. They have scoured the deepest reaches of the Earth's forests and the tallest peaks of faraway mountains.

Still, even though some have returned with compelling evidence, such as casts of footprints, hair samples or even semi-decent video footage, nobody has been able to fully prove the existence of these beings. But how could that be?

If the eyewitness reports are real, and large, ape-like creatures live in remote areas around the globe, we would except to find something more tangible — like a dwelling place or the remains of a dead specimen.

While most cryptid enthusiasts camp out in mountainous forests hoping to catch a glimpse of the strange creature, one possibility seems to have eluded the majority: Bigfoot and the others may live most of their lives underground. Sure, the hairy hominids seem to search forests and mountainsides for food and other resources, but there are many clues that point towards them being mostly subterranean.

For example, consider the Native American tales of Sasquatch that go back long before European settlers even imagined the creature's existence. Some tribes, like the Mono Peoples of Sierra Nevada, California, consider the creatures to be fellow inhabitants of the land. Through generational teachings, they understand that the intelligent beast-men live in the caves and tunnels that run beneath the Sierra region, and only come out on rare occasions.

The idea of these creatures being largely subterranean also fits nicely with the reports of them being mostly nocturnal. Unlike humans, they seem to have no trouble seeing and moving about at night. Eyes like that would most likely be well-fitted for underground living as well. Combine all of this with the fact that most Bigfoot sightings have taken place in, or around, a mountainous area, and this theory seems to make a lot of sense.

With this in mind, perhaps cryptozoologists would be well-advised to examine not only remote forests and mountain ranges, but also the vast, unexplored caves and tunnels that lie underneath them. While this would certainly require more effort and additional safety measures, who knows what could be found in the deeper places of the Earth?

One thing is for certain, however: sightings of Bigfoot and the others are still being reported to this day. With ever-improving, easily-accessible technology, hopes are high that we will eventually get to know the elusive ape-men of our world.

Printed in Great Britain
by Amazon